"Turbulence is the price you pay for flying high, so whenever you're flying high, you're going to have some bumpy areas. Don't give up, hang in there."

-Bishop J. Dew Sheard

The Trailblazer:

My Mathematical Journey

Telashay Swope-Farr, Ph.D.

Foreword By: Elizabeth Drame, Ph.D.

This book is dedicated to Mommy, Daddy, & my Grandparents (The Swopes)

The Trailblazer: My Mathematical Journey

Copyright © 2023 by Telashay Swope-Farr

All rights reserved. Published by SPC Publishing. This book or any portion thereof may not be reproduced or used in any manner whatsoever without the author's express written permission except for the use of brief quotations in a book review.

1. BIOGRAPHY & AUTOBIOGRAPHY /Cultural, Ethnic & Regional / African American & Black
2. BIOGRAPHY & AUTOBIOGRAPHY/Educators
3. BIOGRAPHY & AUTOBIOGRAPHY/Women

Cover Design by: Carlaseea Shannon

Photography Credits: Telashay Swope-Farr

ISBN: 979-8-9877901-2-0

Printed in the United States of America

CONTENTS

Introduction 1

Chapter 1: Her Future 2

   How Mommy Felt About Me 3

   Dr. Swope in the Making 5

Chapter 2: Unknown Mathematician 7

   High School Math 7

      Ticket to Rust 12

Chapter 3: Uncharted Territory 17

   Math Role Model 17

   Math Professor in View 19

Chapter 4: Black Woman Mathematician 25

   Turning Point 28

   Praxis II Dilemma 30

   The Kale Episode 32

Chapter 5: A Dream Come True 36

   Living The Dream 37

   Back to Basics 39

   Ph.D.: Year One 44

      Spring 2017 47

      Summer 2017 49

Ph.D.: Year Two 50
    Spring 2018 51
    Angel in Disguise 52
Ph.D.: Year Three 53
    Disintegration 57
    Spring 2019 58
    Summer 2019 63
Ph.D.: Year Four 65
    Spring 2020: Energized 70
    Living in Ghana 70
    Tourist Attractions 73
    COVID-19 Pandemic 81
Ph.D.: Year Five 84
    Data Collection 85
    Spring 2021 86
Chapter 6: Life After Ph.D. 91
    "Motivationalist" 93
    Conclusion 95
About the Author 97
Acknowledgments 99

Foreword

Elizabeth Drame, Ph.D.
Professor

An anomaly. A rarity. One in a sea of many. The one. The only.

All of these terms can be applied to Black female math educators. While 76.5% of the total teaching population in the U.S. is female, only 6.5% of the total teaching force is Black (U.S. Department of Education, 2020). Among the percentage of educators who teach in the area of math or computer science, the distribution of Black teachers is similarly limited. Only 6.2% of the total percentage of teachers in math for Computer Sciences is Black (Ibid). Among those with advanced degrees, only 1.2% possess a doctorate.

Dr. Telashay Swope-Farr can be seen by some to be that rare anomaly. As a Black woman sitting in various math classes throughout her academic career, Telashay was oftentimes the only Black person in the room, learning from mostly white teachers. Many times, these educators subconsciously operated with implicit biases guiding their actions leading Telashay to navigate negative deficit-oriented ideas about her ability and capacity to learn math.

I first met Telashay five years ago when she reached out to me to learn more about doing research abroad at the recommendation of her doctoral advisor at the time. Telashay wanted to research the African continent and wanted to learn about my experience conducting research in Senegal, West Africa. That initial meeting led to an invitation to serve on her committee as a person who would bring the urban education perspective to her dissertation committee. Looking back on this, I realized that she needed to not be the only one in the room yet again.

I related to her experience of being the only one. As the only Black student in my doctoral program at an Ivy League university, I experienced a level of marginalization and invisibility that is difficult to describe. No one was mean to me. No one was explicitly racist to me. However, they did not see me as someone to be nurtured. They did not see me as a future colleague with whom they could collaborate. They did not understand my research focus and did not place much value on my topic and approach. The feedback was minimal, and I was often left questioning if I was doing the right thing or if I was totally off track. I watched my peers participate in professors' research projects, go to conferences and publish with these same professors while I was left on the sidelines. This experience led me to doubt my place in the academy.

While I was not in the field of math education, my experience in a field where there were few to no Black students was unfortunately a familiar one. When I came into the academy five years after earning my doctorate, I vowed to ensure that no other Black student experienced being unseen or devalued. When Telashay reached out to me to ask me to serve on her committee, it was an enthusiastic yes! I did not have to know much about math education to value what Telashay wanted to bring to the field about understanding how early socialization and educational experiences influenced math educators' efficacy, capacity, and ability to teach math well.

Telashay was an extremely hard worker — driven, ambitious, committed, and ready. By the time we got to her dissertation proposal defense, Telashay was still all these things but also riddled with anxiety and self-doubt. This came not from her skill or capacity but from many interactions over the course of years with white professors, which made her question herself and her pathway.

The transition from student to Dr. can be a bumpy one but those of us who have made the transition need to do everything we can to make it smoother for those who come after us. This does not mean that we lower our expectations or teach and coach with less rigor. Rather, we have an intimate understanding of how challenging this transition can be, and we have a responsibility to reduce the harm that others experience in the process. When the person who is supposed to be in your corner becomes a source of stress and doubt, something needs to give. I stepped in as the lead of Telashay's dissertation committee, and we kept it moving forward. Keeping it moving also meant incorporating some space to breathe, heal and recover.

Telashay's math journey to Dr. Swope captures many highs and lows in a story form that is relatable to many. You can easily picture the persistent girl who would ask a million questions before leaving her algebra class. You can easily picture the stressed dissertator, searching for the 100th article that would prove a particular assertion she was making. I felt alone when I was going through my doctoral journey. If I had Telashay's book, I would have known that I was not alone and that there were other Black women out there who could understand what I was experiencing. Her book would have helped me, and her book will help many others to come!

Introduction

Everyone has a story to tell; mine just happened to be one that unintentionally impacted the lives of many. I would have never fathomed that having the desire to help others learn math would be so influential. As a child, my mother called me a "go-getter"; I always performed well. Unknowingly this success was paving the way for my rewarding future. When it came to learning mathematics, I excelled at every grade level. Yet it never dawned on me that I was good at math. As I reflected on learning math, it came naturally. However, my natural math ability halted when I began graduate school to obtain a master's in mathematics. Learning math was so challenging for the first time that I second-guessed all my math knowledge and proficiency. This experience birthed my mathematical journey and life as a trailblazer. God was preparing me for something I could not handle at that time.

This book tells the story of the many challenges I faced to reach my goal of becoming Dr. Swope, from experiencing math success to what felt like consistent failures. Along with the highs and lows of learning the ins and outs of graduate school, I ultimately prevailed by God's grace. I became the first Black graduate student at the University of Wisconsin-Milwaukee to earn a Ph.D. in urban education specializing in mathematics education. As I endured many obstacles, I hoped I was paving the way for many who also dream of becoming someone great.

Chapter 1: Her Future

When it comes to success, anyone can accomplish anything if they are intrinsically motivated. As an overachiever, I was fueled by self-motivation to have a prosperous future, and my stepfather, Terry Shannon, was my most significant encourager. At a very young age, my dad told me I would attend college to be an engineer. Of course, as a young girl, I had no clue what an engineer was or what it took to become one. Nonetheless, his consistent talk about me attending college sparked the desire to fulfill his dreams.

When he met my mother, who was pregnant with me, he fell in love with me and had my future planned. Daddy told mommy I was going to college, and mommy wondered how he knew this. Daddy explained, "because I went, she's going too." Daddy continued to say, "and she's going to be good at math and intelligent just like me." How could he know this even before I was born? Some faith and confidence he must have had.

As a child, Daddy consistently said I had to attend college. He said it so frequently that I never thought I had other options. College-bound was what it would be by any means necessary. The funny thing is, although Daddy had this requirement, one would think he would have prepared for it, but he did not. There were no college savings, tours, or any college exposure. As I entered middle and high school, my mind and heart focused on going to college. I heard of a college tour called In Roads and wanted to participate, but I did not have access to the information nor knew how to obtain it. Nevertheless, that did not change my aspiration to attend college.

Out of thin air, I developed this yearning to attend a Historically Black College/University (HBCU). I heard that one of my older cousins went to Tennessee State University (TSU), an HBCU in Nashville, TN; he did not graduate. I began to set my heart on TSU. Had I visited TSU, seen or researched any information about them, or even talked with my cousin about his experience? No, but TSU was where I wanted to be; for all I cared, it was an HBCU, a place I desired to go.

One day it finally dawned on me that my parents had not saved any money for me to go to college. Therefore, my mind went into overdrive, and my intrinsic motivation tripled to figure out how I would be able to afford college. I presumed that if I worked hard to obtain good grades, I might get some scholarships. I thought, what a plan, Dad, you wanted me to go to college but had no finances; how would this work? Maybe he figured it would work out somehow.

How Mommy Felt About Me

Mommy loved me so much that she gave up her dreams of attending college to be a veterinarian after having me. To have a child at the gentle age of sixteen must have been challenging for her. Mommy said,

"I knew I got pregnant at a young age and wanted to go to college to be a vet, but my dreams were shattered because I got pregnant at fifteen. My mother told me if I wanted to go to college, I would have to pay for it myself because I put myself in a woman's position. I had to take care of my child. I always wanted you to go to college and do better than I did. From head start up, I knew you were destined for greatness because you were sincere about everything you did in school. Watching your accomplishments, I knew you were on the right track. Even when you had a hiccup in high school, I knew you would persevere. In every task you started, you always came out on top. Even with the Bible quiz, you always strived for greatness."

Despite Mommy giving up her future to care for me, she was not bitter or disappointed. Instead, she wanted me to achieve those things she could not. Could I meet my mother's expectations and surpass her personal goals? In her eyes, I could, and I did.

Through mommy's eyes, I was the perfect little girl that always made her proud and excelled at every task. Little Miss Perfect experienced a hiccup (as mommy called it) in high school, which could have changed my future. Despite that situation, mommy knew I would stay the course. Thank God, who knew best, that incident worked in my favor, and I was back focused on going to college. Thank God for having such a fantastic mother who believed in me no matter what I did or did not do. She never gave up on me and encouraged me to do my best at everything I set my mind to accomplish.

Dr. Swope in the Making

Traveling to different states was always an activity I enjoyed. I was fortunate to go on summer trips down south with my grandparents when I was young. My maternal grandfather, Preston Swope, who I called daddy also, was from Florence, Alabama. My maternal grandmother, Gladys Swope, Nana, or Momma, as I called her, grew up in Pontotoc, Mississippi. Each summer, my uncle and I spent two weeks with my grandparents, visiting family in each state. Those drives down south were long, but I looked forward to being with my grandparents as they were an integral part of my upbringing, not to mention they had me spoiled. It was my grandfather, Preston Swope, whose family impacted me the most.

One summer in Florence, we visited his cousin Dr. Swope, a veterinarian. I do not recall him telling me much about his career, but the fact that he was a doctor inspired me to be one too. The sound of that name, Dr. Swope, intrigued me, and the dream of becoming Dr. Swope was set in motion that day. I didn't know what it took to earn a doctorate. I did not know what type of doctor I would be, but that did not matter; my heart was set on being Dr. Swope. At no time did I consider how earning a doctorate aligned with being an engineer.

It was not until undergraduate school that I realized becoming an engineer would not be my chosen career path. Learning that majoring in engineering at Rust College meant three years there and two years at another institution was not appealing. Being uninformed about college, I did not know how transferring to another college would work when the three years ended. I was unfamiliar with attending college, although I desperately wanted to go. Instead, I decided to become a math professor, which requires a doctorate, then I would be Dr. Swope. This plan sounded well until I began taking graduate-level math courses and not performing well.

During graduate school, many math professors were older white men who looked weird and bored, as if they spent much time reading math books, conducting research, and calculating math problems. One professor was so strange; he would walk around the hallways without shoes. Having this mindset made me ponder if earning a doctorate in mathematics to be a professor was the best choice for my future. I told myself I would not sit with my face in math books all day; I wanted a life. Further, I knew I did not enjoy reading as it made me sleepy. I was inadequate at reading comprehension; thus, I doubted my ability to comprehend and recall large amounts of information. Therefore, I second-guess the idea of pursuing a doctorate.

Seeing the professors' strange behavior in the math department and my lack of interest in reading impacted my dream of becoming Dr. Swope. One might wonder how other individuals' appearances and possible ways of life could influence my decision to turn away from my childhood dream. It was easy; not knowing about the requirements to obtain a doctorate and not taking the initiative to talk with a math professor about their position made it simple to default to a different option for my future. At that time, I decided to pursue teaching high school mathematics. My dream died, and so did my confidence in mathematics.

Chapter 2: Unknown Mathematician

I hate math; Why do I need to learn math? As long as I can count my money, I don't need to learn math; Algebra—why would they include letters with numbers? These are the comments I often heard when I began teaching math or told someone I was a math teacher. I frequently thought you don't need math; it's hard; you only need to count money.

Math is not complicated and is used in many areas of our lives. Rarely do I initially think about the number of people who may have had unfortunate experiences learning math or may have struggled to understand math content. Therefore, everyone will not like math as much as I do. Strangely I did not realize I was good at math or thrived in it during K–12. I was persistent about ensuring I understood the concepts to obtain good grades.

High School Math

I am sure Mr. Giles was tired of me and could not wait until the bell rang for algebra class to end. Each day, although I had a seat in the front row, I would sit at the empty teacher's desk next to his desk, persistently asking for help. He would say, "Ms. Swope, can you please sit at your desk?" "Yes, Mr. Giles, after you help me with this problem." I'd laugh and keep sitting next to him until I understood the math concepts we were learning that day. I drove Mr. Giles crazy every day, so much so that he had a funny look as I pranced up to his desk to sit next to him for help until I understood my work. It is funny my mother would say, "at least you understand him because he didn't teach me anything when I was in his class. He told us to read the examples in the book." I was a different student than my mother. I made certain teachers earn their paychecks because I would ask a million and one questions until I understood. This theory worked in my favor because I passed Mr. Giles's algebra class with an A.

I wished I had had a similar experience with Mrs. Hacker in my sophomore geometry class. I did not catch onto Mrs. Hacker's instructional methods. No matter how many questions I asked, I could not get the hang of what to do. Unfortunately, I did not pass that class with an A, and I was not too fond of geometry until college. Ironically, I have never taught geometry as a stand-alone subject, and when I am required to teach geometric concepts, I always recall my math experience in Mrs. Hacker's class.

Although I did not perform well mathematically sophomore year in high school, I quickly turned that around during my junior year in Mrs. Kubinski's class. Mrs. Kubinski was one of the best math teachers I ever had. Taking her pre-calculus/trigonometry class was always exciting. She consistently ensured I understood, and her teaching methods made it easy for me to comprehend. I performed so well that others in the class thought I was a genius. My cousin Brandon explained,

> "When I used to come in [class], you'd be sitting at your desk ahead of time. I'd always say, Tela, what's the quadratic formula? You'd always remember all the formulas. You'd

> always help me out. Having you made it easy because we were family."

I must have been moving through high school mindlessly. I had no clue I was doing that well in math and that my math knowledge influenced how other students learned math. It appears I was well known as a superb math student since Malena said, "you were always good at math in high school. I remember you having this fancy calculator with colored gems on it. I wanted a calculator like that too." Lord knows I do not remember having a fancy calculator back then or that Malena also took notice of my math abilities. People were more observant of me than I was of me. My mind was focused on getting the work done to earn good grades. I never really took notice of or reflected on how successful I was. Brandon said,

> "Having you in that class [pre-calculus/trig], you were more attentive, and you wouldn't let people just copy. You made learning fun. Your spirit was so high your energy illuminated the class. You were so smart, stayed on point, and always understood. If you didn't, you'd raise your hand. When it was test time, I used to be like, Swope, I need you; you always helped me out."

I had the slightest idea that Brandon thought of me this way and that I was a mathematician. God was forming me like the potter's clay to be someone with the passion and drive to help individuals improve mathematically.

Overall high school was a blur for me. I finished freshmen year just shy of a 4.0 g.p.a and was in the top ten of my class. My grade point average dropped my sophomore year due to a shift in focus from academics to a boy. After nearly having my life changed forever, I got back on track and graduated with a 3.6 g.p.a. I did so well that I could enroll in co-op, a program that allowed students to leave school early to work for companies that partnered with our high school. Junior year I only had five classes instead of six; therefore, I left school early to work at an accounting office. By senior year, I had earned enough credits to attend school half-days, which allowed me to work two jobs.

While balancing school and work, I never lost sight of my dream to attend an HBCU. Since I had never set foot on any college campus and had no idea what to expect, I thought it would be wise to consult someone with insight into HBCUs. At Mt. Clemens high school, the only black educators were Mr. Jackson—the principal, Mr. Giles, and Ms. Rice—one of two counselors. There were four black educators at the middle school housed in the same building: Mrs. Karim—my math teacher; Mrs. Jackson—my English teacher; Mr. Benson—a science teacher; and Mr. Timberlake—my guidance counselor. Since my last name begins with an S, my high school counselor was Mr. Thomas. He was friendly and sweet; however, I never went to him for post-secondary advice. Ms. Rice was one I thought I should consult with about attending an HBCU.

One day while visiting her office, I explained my eagerness to attend an HBCU, and she explicitly shared the pros and cons. I recall her saying,

"Telashay, going to an HBCU is nice. You'll see a lot of students like you. However, the facilities won't be as pleasant as those at a predominantly white institution (PWI). The dormitories will not be as nice and comfortable, and they may not have air conditioners, but you will get a good education. It is best to apply to as many schools as possible just in case you aren't accepted to the college you want to attend. And to help with college application fees, I will give you some fee waivers."

I was so happy I visited Ms. Rice that day; I was more eager than before to embark on my college journey and apply to TSU.

Since I had a few college application fee waivers, I wanted to adhere to Ms. Rice's advice. I applied to Michigan State University (MSU), TSU, and Eastern Michigan University. I was accepted to MSU and Eastern, but not TSU. Receiving that news broke my heart, and I was a little discouraged. Still, I figured getting accepted into MSU was an honor since it was a top-ten Michigan university. Why not be happy about that? It could have been the case that no college accepted me. Despite the dispiritedness, I still wanted to fulfill my dream of attending an HBCU. Therefore, my Nana advised me to call her high school friend Mr. Bates, to learn about a different HBCU, Tuskegee University in Alabama. I do not recall where the idea of going to Tuskegee came from, but I was determined to find an HBCU.

Ticket to Rust

I called Mr. Bates, and what a conversation that was. I explained my longing to attend an HBCU and how I wanted to learn about Tuskegee since TSU did not accept me. Mr. Bates said that's a good college, but let me tell you about Rust College, my alma mater. He began to sing, "Oh, the world is full of colleges, but there's one that is my own..." That was the first line of Rust College's school song. I giggled as he finished since Mr. Bates was a good singer. He said, "and I know you would do good at Rust. You should call Mr. McDonald, the admissions counselor; I'm sure they can find a scholarship for an intelligent girl like you." Ok, Mr. Bates, I'll call him, not knowing what to expect but hoping the outcome would be favorable. Mr. Bates said, "call me back and tell me how it went. If you come down to Holly Springs, I'll take good care of you and make a lovely quilt, especially for you."

I gave Mr. McDonald a call right away. I explained my desire to attend an HBCU and told him my g.p.a, and immediately he said, "Well, Ms. Swope, I will send you an acceptance letter and give you a presidential scholarship which includes tuition, room, and board for all four years." My eyes instantly filled with tears. I hung up the phone and screamed, "THANK YOU, JESUS!!! I'm going to Rust College, an HBCU." Strangely, I had not spoken with my parents first to get their permission, for I assumed they would be ok with the news and my decision to go. I did not research anything about Rust College, what they are known for, the types of programs offered, or what the campus or residence halls look like. I was so excited that I never thought about these critical elements.

August 2001 came, and it was time to head to Holly Springs, MS, for freshmen orientation. I packed up everything I had in my bedroom, loaded Nana's van, and Mommy, Nana, I hit 94 west for Mississippi. One might wonder why my number one cheerleader, Daddy, did not accompany us; I cannot recall, especially since he and Mommy were no longer married. However, I believe he was cheering me on from Michigan.

That 12-hour drive was familiar since I had been used to going to Mississippi during the summers. This time I would have a more extended stay than before. As we approached the Holly Springs/Oxford exit (exit 30) off highway 78, I felt excitement and anticipation about what the college campus looked like. The campus was not too far from the exit as Holly Springs was a tiny town with very few stores or places for entertainment. About three minutes from campus, we drove through what southerners call the town square, a part of town that forms a square with businesses on each side. I looked out the window and wondered where in the world I was. I had never seen such a small town that gave off an ancient feel. I continued silently riding until we turned right onto Rust Ave, then left onto campus.

The campus was a big circle that appeared to be one way on and one way off. The administration building, the A building as we called it, sat vertically from the main entrance. Then to the right of the A building was the cafeteria housed inside the mass communications building. We turned right, passed these buildings, and quickly left to arrive at E.L. Rust Hall, the residence for freshmen girls. This hall was to the right of the campus post office, where I loved to visit since I received many encouraging letters and cards. We parked and headed into E. L. Rust, and instantly, all the excitement I once felt diminished.

When we walked through glass doors to enter the dorm, it wreaked an unbearable odor. I proceeded into a tiny office to check in with the residence hall director to receive my room assignment and key. She directed me to the hallway leading to a small two-person room that maybe only a fourth of my items could hold. Tears began to form in my eyes as I thought about my decision to attend this college. My mind instantly went back to my conversation with Ms. Rice, some HBCUs are not up to par, and this one certainly fits that description. While the tears continued to flow, I looked at Mommy and Nana and said, I can't do this. I was so used to living in a two-bedroom house, basically alone. How could I survive in this smelly dorm in a tiny room for two people with two restrooms on a hallway for at least thirty females? Nana said, "Telabee get in the van, and we will go home." Nana, I can't go back home; I turned down MSU to come here. What will I do instead? I exclaimed. These thoughts came from a novice college student who had no idea what I could have done about getting readmitted to MSU. Neither did I know I should have written a letter to TSU to learn why I was not admitted even though I had an acceptable g.p.a. Three years later, while visiting the math department at TSU, I found that I should have inquired about why I was not accepted.

The Trailblazer: My Mathematical Journey

Feeling inexperienced, I swallowed my pride, wiped my tears away, and headed to the van to grab my belongings to set up my new home for the next four years. Being the spoiled brat I was, instead of staying on campus during freshman orientation, I decided to stay at Mr. Bates's house with my family. I figured I would enjoy any luxury I could before I had to live on campus. Mr. Bates thought that was a bad idea; he felt I needed to get used to being on campus. But Nana said, "let my baby stay with me." Oh, how I loved my Nana. She always knew how to make me happy. I stayed at Mr. Bates during freshmen orientation and mustered up the courage to say goodbye to my family so I could move onto campus. The sweet deal was Mr. Bates made me a nine-patch quilt for my bed as a welcome gift to help me feel nice and cozy while living in the dorm. Mr. Bates was a man of his word; he took great care of me all four years. He allowed me to stay at his house on the weekends and prepared the best home-cooked meals that featured the world's best mac n cheese.

Although my first experience visiting a college campus was the day I moved into a residence hall, I quickly became acquainted with college life. I learned how to deal with circumstances I was not used to, not having access to the luxuries from home, and to make the best of all situations. After settling at Rust College, one of the first decisions I had to make was declaring a major. Although I wanted to make daddy proud by becoming an engineer, I had given up on this career path. Unfortunately, I did not know what to study, so I declared an undecided major freshman year.

One day while sitting in a math course, I realized I should be a math professor. It was in my heart to help students understand math concepts better and have a different learning experience while improving their math confidence. I wanted them to develop an appreciation for math and change their feelings about the subject. I believed I had what it took to produce math aces. A math ace is an individual who excels at mathematics when given the proper attention and tools needed to succeed. Often math educators do not teach math well, although they have excellent math knowledge. Having math knowledge does not equate to the ability to teach mathematical concepts effectively. With this in mind, my math journey to affect change in the mathematics community began.

Chapter 3: Uncharted Territory

Imagine going on a trip, your bags are packed, the car is filled with gas, you put the car in drive, and then you realize you do not know how to reach your destination. You desire to go out of town but have not determined the best route. Sounds silly, right? Especially since you prepared for the trip. Nonetheless, this was how I began my college journey but in reverse. I knew I was going to college, but I never took the time to research potential programs or different career options. Neither did I do this during my freshmen year of college while declaring an undecided major. During my freshmen year, I was placed in an entry-level math course. Some colleges require students to take an entrance exam to determine the courses needed for their first year, but not Rust College; at least, I was not required to do so. Luckily my math knowledge was above average, so the instructor allowed me to take the next level math course since the freshman-level course was too easy. Mr. McCoy, one of the best math advisors I ever had, was the math instructor. He instantly recognized that I had been inaccurately placed into his freshman-level math course and suggested I take his geometry course instead.

Math Role Model

Less than 8% of mathematicians are Black/African American. We are extremely rare in the field of mathematics. To have a black math instructor was inspiring, and he thought highly of me. I am sure Mr. McCoy would have never imagined his impact on me naturally and mathematically. He was a fantastic math instructor who ensured I understood all the concepts he presented; when I did not, he encouraged me to keep taking notes. I was the type of student who would not write down anything if I did not comprehend the concept right away. Mr. McCoy would say, "you will understand it one day, even better when you have to teach it." If I can't understand it now, how can I teach it to someone else? It was challenging to take notes if I did not understand the material. Before leaving the class, I needed to know every procedure satisfactorily to boost my confidence so I would not struggle with homework.

Mr. McCoy never allowed me to sit in his class and not get my notes written, for he would fuss at me until I began writing the examples. His desire for me to stay current with note-taking became a method I used with my students. I consistently encourage them to get their notes down even when they struggle to understand so they have something to refer back to while studying and completing homework.

Most of my math courses were with Mr. McCoy, some of which gave me headaches. The math was so complex that I would check out during instruction and whine. Nonetheless, Mr. McCoy always encouraged me to focus and push through. I needed to take a few higher-level math courses that Mr. McCoy did not have the credentials to teach. Therefore, the mathematics department chair, Dr. Yeh, sought an external instructor. No matter who taught a math course I had to take, Mr. McCoy was always available to help when I struggled to understand. He was so supportive that when I graduated and decided to retake the Praxis II test, my husband and I drove to Mississippi from Wisconsin for him to help me. When I needed college transcripts, I called Mr. McCoy and asked him to go to the registrar's office, pick them up, and mail them to me. He was always happy to do it and excited to hear from me.

Mr. McCoy has been an influential part of my math journey; he significantly impacted my decision to become a math educator. He unquestionably inspired me to be a math mentor to any student needing math support. Mr. McCoy told me as a black woman in math, I would never be without a job. Back then, I did not know there were a small number of black women math professors and teachers and how priceless they are in mathematics.

Mr. McCoy saw something in me and, without exception, motivated me to do well mathematically. As an integral part of my life, he helped me recognize my math abilities. He was a man of wisdom, for many things he shared with me came to fruition. One example was understanding math better once I began teaching. Taking the time to prepare math lessons and practice the math before teaching it to my students gave me a depth of understanding I did not have when I learned some math concepts. With gratitude, I honor Mr. McCoy as the true definition of a role model and mentor.

Math Professor in View

During sophomore year, I became a mathematics major. I was excelling in all math courses except one, differential equations. The concepts were confusing, which could have been due to the instructional methods used. The professor was foreign, it was difficult to understand his English, and he did not do a good job helping me understand the concepts in general. Of course, I asked many questions and rarely wrote down examples because I could not grasp his explanations. Indeed, Mr. McCoy would not have been happy to know that, but this instructor did not have the skills for teaching that Mr. McCoy had.

I performed so poorly in differential equations that Dr. Yeh talked with the professor about ensuring I successfully passed the course. Doing so showed that even Dr. Yeh was aware of my math abilities. Although I passed that class with a C, the only C I had ever earned at Rust College, I learned nothing. I was highly disappointed with my grade and the lack of knowledge I had. It felt like I finished that math course without learning anything, and I was just assigned a grade. Be that as it may, taking that course fueled my desire to become a math professor even more. I vowed to try my hardest to ensure students understood the concepts I would teach them and help them feel comfortable learning math. With this commitment in mind, I thought it would be a good idea to change my major to mathematics education to learn what it took to be a good teacher and the best pedagogical skills for math instruction.

I made the switch to mathematics education and jumped right into education courses. Human Growth and Development was the course I remember most. Mrs. Stovall, a lovely and distinctive black woman, taught that course; she was hilarious. She'd make faces while sliding her readers from her head to her face, then to the tip of her nose, back and forth while teaching about family dynamics and how humans develop from early adolescence through adolescents. Mrs. Stovall was so animated that I enjoyed being in the class to witness her actions more than learning about children.

Teaching Strategies Practicum was a second memorable class, but not nearly as memorable as Mrs. Stovall's. In this course, we learned about different styles of pedagogy. During this time, I had to take the Praxis I exam. Praxis I is an exam that assesses the knowledge and skills needed to prepare for the classroom. It is composed of reading, writing, and math. This exam is known to be easy, and the Praxis II was said to be even easier since it assesses an individual's subject expertise. As luck would have it, the Praxis I was challenging for me. I took it twice and did not earn adequate scores on the reading and writing portions. I felt dumb as if I could not read or write. However, that was not the case. I believe test anxiety was an issue, especially since it was a timed test. After failing twice, I changed my mind about majoring in mathematics education and switched back to mathematics. I told myself this was not for me, which was reasonable since I did not want to teach K–12 grade anyway. My heart was set on teaching college-level students.

I felt like Katherine Johnson, who said, *"it's not everyday you wake up with a mission and I was determined to accomplish it."* This time, I decided to stick with pure mathematics and set my sights on graduate school to obtain a doctorate. I thought there would be no more stumbling blocks, for I was on a mission to achieve my goals. All began well as I continued taking math courses with Mr. McCoy. I enjoyed them because most of the attention was on me since there were usually two of us in class—myself and Kamiah, who later became my best friend. He was also a math major and on the men's basketball team, where I served as team manager. We spent countless hours in the library completing math homework and studying for exams together. With such small math classes, I was fortunate to get the one-on-one attention necessary to pass most math courses with an A.

There were two courses that Mr. McCoy was unavailable to teach—Linear Algebra, taught by Mr. Sesei, and Number Theory, taught by Mr. Ritch. I also did well in these classes and enjoyed Mr. Sesei's class. He was from Africa and very funny. Although I was sailing through my math courses and enjoying my instructors, this honeymoon phase suddenly stopped.

None of the math instructors could teach the next level of required math courses at Rust. No one was qualified, meaning one had to have a certain number of graduate-level credits in mathematics or a master's in mathematics. Not having qualified math instructors could have been the case because there were no mathematics majors in seven years; no one had graduated with a mathematics degree. What would I do? I had come close to finishing my degree, and now I had another issue. Thankfully having God on my side, there was a solution. Dr. Yeh pleaded with the dean of instruction to hire someone externally to teach Kamiah and I. The dean permitted Dr. Yeh to search for someone, and he found a seasoned black male math instructor willing to teach us Abstract Algebra I and II. I did pretty well in these courses, passing with a B and an A, respectively. After getting over this last hurdle, I was on the home stretch as I began to prepare to graduate with a Bachelor of Science in mathematics.

I was overwhelmingly excited on April 24, 2005, because I was one of two students to graduate with a mathematics degree. Not only did I complete the first step of my goal to become a math professor, but I also finished with Magna Cum Laude honors and as a member of Alpha Kappa Mu national honors society. I was elated to be the first person in my family to attend and complete college. I made daddy so proud, and his words were, "I knew you would do it; I'm so proud of you. That's my baby."

Having four years of a college experience, I was better prepared to apply for graduate school. Having test anxiety, I searched for graduate schools that did not require the graduate records exam (GRE). The GRE is a standardized test that assesses one's readiness for graduate school. I did not want to take any chances of not being able to attend graduate school because I struggled with standardized tests. I initially searched for schools in Michigan and found Oakland University (OU). OU was close to home, so I applied and was accepted. Due to my participation in an internship at The University of Akron with the McNair Scholars program, I applied for the Advanced Opportunity Program (AOP) fellowship at OU. I was awarded the fellowship, which included tuition for four years and a monthly stipend to fund my financial obligations.

Shortly after my acceptance to OU, I was reunited with a teenage crush from church. Apelles was always fond of me and finally became serious about making me his wife; as a result, we became engaged. Since he was from Milwaukee, I decided to search for a university in Milwaukee that did not require the GRE and had fellowship opportunities. Someone once told me, "If you pay for graduate school, you did not do your homework." Therefore, I was adamant about securing financial assistance, especially since I had given up the fellowship I secured at OU. I applied to The University of Wisconsin-Milwaukee (UWM) and for the AOP fellowship offered by the graduate school. Divine favor was on my side; I was accepted into the master's program for mathematics and received the AOP fellowship. This AOP fellowship consisted of four-year tuition, a monthly stipend, and free health insurance. Additionally, I was not charged for out-of-state tuition since I was not a Wisconsin resident.

Chapter 4: Black Woman Mathematician

"Girls are capable of doing everything men are capable of doing."
-Katherine Johnson

Earning a graduate degree in mathematics is no easy task. Try being a black woman seeking such a degree. Mr. McCoy told me I would be a hot commodity when I finished school, but he neglected to tell me how challenging this pursuit would be. According to Marjorie Brown, "it was extremely unusual for a black woman to earn a bachelor's degree in math in the 1940s." She was one of the first African American women to earn a Ph.D. She explained that it was even more unusual for them to take it further and pursue graduate work. Although it was sixty-five years later when I began working toward my graduate degree, that ideology was still valid.

When I began pursuing a master's in mathematics, it was difficult. Due to my undergraduate success in math, I was advised to take challenging math courses that I could not handle. At Rust, we had modules that lasted eight weeks. Therefore, instead of taking a course for sixteen weeks, an entire semester, I had courses for eight weeks then I would begin new courses. Thus, I had the advantage of taking more math courses each semester. Although I was exposed to many math concepts, I only received a breadth of knowledge versus a depth of knowledge, which ultimately disadvantaged me mathematically in graduate school.

Attending classes was very uncomfortable, and I realized I could not keep up with or understand the material. I spent lots of money on books and time trying to figure out what courses I should take that would be manageable for me to comprehend. I would enroll in courses, sit in them for a few days, then drop them because the material was too advanced. I often found myself in the department chair's office, attempting to ascertain what to do. No manual was available to inform students of what courses were required to obtain a master's in math, nor was I assigned an advisor like I was accustomed to at Rust. I asked Dr. Stone, the department chair if a need sheet (course list/credits) was available so I could determine the courses I needed to take. He was clueless about what I was referring to and finally told me there were three options to obtain a master's in math: 24 credit option, 30 credit option, and 36 credit option. The fewer credit options encompass higher-level courses. For example, if students chose the 24-credit option, they would take fewer courses, but these courses would be more advanced. After explaining these choices, Dr. Stone suggested I find an advisor to help me. I was dumbfounded because I was already struggling with course selection; how would I know which professor would be best to advise me? I was unclear about the process, and he did not take the time to guide me. He said, "find an expert professor in the subject you are interested in studying." I thought, ok, sir, at this point, how would I know what subject I am interested in being new to graduate school? Doesn't graduate school help decide what a student becomes interested in studying? Further, how would I know each professor's interest that information was not posted outside their office?

The Trailblazer: My Mathematical Journey

I was at a dead end, or at least it felt like it, until I went to Dr. Jeb Willenbring's office hours. He taught one of the courses I was having difficulty with. I told him my situation and wondered if he could provide any advice. Dr. Jeb said, "it sounds like you need to improve your math proof skills since you have not taken many courses that require proofs. Why don't you sign up for my math 341 course, and I'll make sure you do well." Dr. Jeb reminded me of Mr. McCoy. He saw I needed guidance and was willing to ensure I did not give up on graduate school. He also suggested I take two other lower-level math courses for which I could earn graduate credits and boost my math confidence and abilities. I certainly appreciated that talk with Dr. Jeb because I had lost my confidence in math, believing that I must not have learned enough at Rust to do well in graduate school.

I enrolled in math 341 — Intro to the Language and Practice of Mathematics, Linear Programming, and Introduction to Statics I. Dr. Gervini taught Statistics I; I remember him well because he was friendly and helpful during office hours. My experiences with these professors intensified my desire to become a math professor. They showed me that although I felt unsupported, they were a few good caring professors. Some professors can be unwelcoming and unapproachable, making students feel incapable of learning. While other professors are helpful and caring, fostering an inviting environment.

At UWM, the mathematics department was filled with predominately white male professors. Ironically, one female math professor made me feel incapable of grasping the concepts covered in her course. I had her for differential equations, and when I attended her office hours, she did not explain the material in a way I could understand. She rushed through the explanations as if she did not have time to ensure I understood. I thought she would have been more nurturing and supportive since I was also a woman trying to learn mathematics and become a math professor too. Although I did not share my desire to become a math professor with her, I felt she could have explained concepts more understandably so I could successfully pass her course. Maybe I was not the kind of student she took an interest in or cared enough to assist. Maybe it was the subject, differential equations, since I had struggled with that course at Rust.

Turning Point

Despite my initial setback, taking lower-level math courses, I did well but never regained the math confidence I once had at Rust. To add insult to injury, I was not embraced well in the math department. When I walked through the halls and used the math department office, I detected a sense of unbelonging. I recall going into the office one day to make a copy and look for supplies when one of the secretaries said, "excuse me, can I help you with something? What are you doing in here?" These questions appear simple and innocent; however, the tone of her voice and the look on her face made me feel uneasy. It was as if I did not belong, or she was surprised to see a black student in the math department. Maybe she was shocked because I was the only black student I'd seen. I explained that I was a graduate student and had a fellowship; thus, I was told I could utilize items and the copy machine. Explaining the situation only prompted an, oh, as if she was in disbelief.

Shortly after this incident, I learned from a graduate student that I not only had access to the math department office, but I should have also received a workspace in one of the graduate student offices and a mailbox. I could not believe no one shared this information with me, and once again, I felt uninformed. However, I sought to obtain what other graduate students were entitled to and was given office space and a mailbox. I finally began feeling part of the mathematics department and thought I would get the hang of graduate school mathematics.

I completed the first semester with decent grades but did not feel like the efficient math student I was in high school and undergraduate school. I was not used to struggling in math and earning Bs and Cs. Obtaining a master's in math was something I could not handle, or maybe I was not intelligent enough or up for the challenge. Therefore, I had to figure out an alternative plan.

While in Dr. Jeb's class, I met a lady named Tamika who told me about a program called MACSTEP in the School of Education. This program would allow me to earn a certification for licensure to teach 6–12 grade math and a master's degree in Curriculum and Instruction (C&I). My mind instantly went back to when I was majoring in mathematics education and all the credits I received that could help if I switched to that program. I was thankful for the information and offered to help her with math homework a few times.

Instead of jumping into the program the following semester, I decided to finish the school year in the math department and took three more math courses. Even though I was excited about earning a master's in a different area rather than giving up on graduate school, I was not happy about taking the Praxis I test again. Test anxiety is not a good feeling, especially since I knew I was smart and could read and write. I later discovered that standardized tests are designed to assess specific skills and abilities, not necessarily one's ability to read, write, or solve math problems. I attempted to suppress my fears and jump into retaking the exam.

Praxis II Dilemma

After failing the reading and writing portion of the praxis I twice, I was exempt from retaking it and moved on to the Praxis II exam (content area exam). The Praxis II exam assesses an individual's subject area knowledge in preparation for teaching. I was confident I could pass the first time since many said focusing on one's specialized subject area would be more straightforward. To pass, I needed to score 135 or higher.

My assurance about passing the Praxis II test disappeared after receiving my score. I missed the required score by twelve points. My mind immediately converted to the many times I had taken Praxis I and failed. After taking the Praxis II three times and failing, I believed I was not as bright in math as I thought, although my grades had shown differently. I purchased all sorts of content-related math material I scored low on and studied harder. This strategy proved useless because I took the test two more times and failed; my score fluctuated up and down. I spent hundreds of dollars taking that test and buying study materials. Finally, I considered getting a personal tutor to brush up on math knowledge I had forgotten or never learned.

I contacted Mr. McCoy to see if he would tutor me, and he agreed. Therefore, my husband and I drove to Holly Springs, 675 miles one way, just to get tutored by Mr. McCoy. I was sure I would earn a passing score if I worked with him. If luck were authentic, I would have the worst of it because working with Mr. McCoy did not help me earn an acceptable score; this was my sixth time taking the test. I tried one more time and failed. After that, I vowed I would not be a high school math teacher and was through with the Praxis test; defeat was an understatement at that point.

Seven months later, out of the blue, I was moved to register for the test again. My first thought was, no way, I'm not putting myself through all that studying and failing again; this is not for me. I even said it was not God's will for me to be a teacher; otherwise, I would have passed the test long ago. I had consistently failed that test for three years. But, in response to my thoughts, the Holy Spirit said, "retake the test, do not tell anyone, and don't study; only familiarize yourself with your graphing calculator." Being in myself, I thought this was an impractical idea, yet the Holy Spirit spoke to me, and I needed to take heed. I did as instructed and realized later that God was testing my faith. Hebrews 11:1 says, "Now faith is the substance of things hoped for, the evidence of things not seen" (KJV). I did not see myself successfully passing the Praxis II exam, but God was using that experience to teach me about faith and trusting Him.

While at work, I received an email from the Educational Testing Service with my test results. My heart began to pound, and nervousness took over my body, but I proceeded to check for my score. I was surprised to see a score of 141. Tears of joy began to roll down my face because I not only passed but exceeded the required score by six points. Thank You, Jesus, is all I could say, for I was pleased and in disbelief. After years of trying to earn an acceptable score, I finally passed and learned a spiritual lesson. Putting faith in God and trusting Him when he gives instructions is essential. God received all the glory in that situation. This experience showed I could not pass the Praxis II test alone; I needed God's divine assistance.

While it had been two years since I finished my master's degree, I had not completed the teacher certification portion due to unsuccessful completion of the Praxis II test. I could now submit my score to the C&I department to complete the MACSTEP program and apply for my math certification. Passing the Praxis II test was only one hurdle I accomplished. Another challenge was dealing with my C&I advisor Dr. Kale.

The Kale Episode

An advisor provides advice and guides a student while obtaining a degree. The issue with this definition is that not every individual who wears an advisor's hat upholds that title well. Dr. Barry Kale was my advisor when I transferred to the C&I program. He was an older white man, like a math god at UWM and in the mathematics community. Even though he was a math guru, I struggled to learn from him because he was an abstract educator. He had been in education longer than I had been alive and was well respected for his wealth of knowledge in mathematics. Although I passed his math methods courses with A-, I did not retain much information. Unfortunately, having math smarts does not always translate well when teaching students.

One day Dr. Kale came to observe me teach during my student teaching practicum and provided vague and unhelpful feedback. I did not have the luxury of having a cooperating teacher like others completing their student teaching practicum. I was already a high school math teacher. Since Dr. Kale was my advisor, I expected him to provide specific feedback that would help improve my instruction and inform me of what I was doing well. He told me, "your teaching style is very dry." My immediate thoughts were, how would I improve in this area? What did I do wrong? Was there anything acceptable about my instructional practices? Without a cooperating teacher, I had no one to provide guidance or serve as a model to gain ideas or learn best instructional practices.

Dr. Kale made me feel useless like I was not a good teacher or had room for growth. During his math methods courses, I did not recall any suggested pedagogical methods that proved successful in teaching high school students. He never referred me to any after he visited my class. The only thing I recalled him lecturing on was various math concepts. One concept I remember most was multiplying polynomials. We discussed strategies for multiplying binomials, and he forbade the FOIL method — multiplying the First, Outer, Inner, and Last terms of the binomials. I believe his reasoning for banning the FOIL method was that it focused more on the process (procedures) than understanding the concept. Nonetheless, Dr. Kale came to mind every time I taught this concept.

Near the end of my master's program, I enrolled in a master's seminar course. Students could take it in place of completing a master's thesis. This course helped students prepare a research paper similar to a thesis, but it was not defended in front of a graduate committee, only presented to the course professor and class. Since I was the only black female mathematician that used to be in the math department at that time, I thought it would be interesting to research the rarity of African American female mathematicians. However, Dr. Kale did not believe that was an ideal topic; he believed there was no shortage of African American women in math, and that's how he left it. He did not offer any suggested topics or speak on current trends in the field of math. Fortunately, my professor for the course said, "research what is interesting to you, not him; it does not matter what he thinks." I was happy she encouraged me to follow my interest, although I felt a lack of guidance and support from Dr. Kale. I had begun to think he did not take me seriously as an advisee. It was almost as if he doubted my ability to be successful.

I researched the scarcity of African American women in math and found a great deal of literature. I even had the opportunity of meeting a famous author at a math conference whose research I used. She assured me my topic was worth pursuing and that I was correct about the low number of black women in math.

Experiencing unpleasant encounters with someone responsible for guiding you through an essential part of your life can be discouraging. You may have feelings of inadequacy, doubt, and despair; nevertheless, you must persevere and have faith in yourself. Further, never let anyone dictate your interest or future, especially when your interest may not align with their views. My experiences earning a master's degree taught me steadfastness amid appalling circumstances. Even when others did not believe in my hopes and dreams, I did not lose heart. I persevered through trying times and believed that God would carry me through.

Chapter 5: A Dream Come True

Becoming a math teacher was my new aspiration. So much so that when an opportunity presented itself to teach high school, I jumped at the chance. I met an engineering instructor while in the math department who informed me that his wife's school, she was a principal, was looking for an algebra teacher. This position was with a charter school with an African-based focus that exposed black students to African culture. I was so anxious to begin teaching that I gave up my fellowship to work full-time. Initially, I thought this was a great idea; however, in hindsight, that decision came as a double-edged sword. While excited about teaching high school math, I incurred thousands of dollars in student loans for the remaining year of my master's degree. I worked at the charter school for two years before transitioning to a public high school in the Milwaukee Public School district (MPS).

HSA was one of the largest high schools in MPS. It served over 1400 students and had a reputation for being a rough school. There were disciplinary concerns with the students, making some teachers fear teaching. I disagreed with the reputation this school had, for what some identified as a rough school was only children being children. The children had disagreements, earned average grades, and behaved like typical high school students.

I enjoyed teaching at this school for the first two years. I was able to make a difference in students' math understanding and build a good rapport with them. Two situations occurred that produced doubt about working there. First, I had not passed the Praxis II exam, which affected my status as a teacher. Not having a teaching certification caused me to be demoted to a long-term substitute until I could obtain a math teaching license. Secondly, I was a part-time instructor for two years at a college and finally got the opportunity to teach full-time. Teaching full-time at Bryant & Stratton College was favorable. I would fulfill my goal of teaching at the collegiate level and earn higher pay since the pay for a long-term substitute was lower than a full-time teacher's salary. Ironically, if I had remained a full-time teacher, my salary would have been higher at MPS than at Bryant & Stratton. As far as I was concerned, money was not a motivator; becoming a math instructor was more important. Before accepting the full-time position at Bryant and Stratton, I passed the Praxis II exam and could have returned to full-time teacher status and salary in MPS. Yet, that was no temptation for me; I followed my heart and accepted the job at the college.

Living The Dream

Teaching college students was exciting. I enjoyed serving adults and helping them gain a better understanding of math. It was always heartwarming when the light bulb went off when they finally comprehended math concepts they had previously struggled to learn. My love and passion for math increased as I worked in the tutoring center and assisted students during lunch breaks. I had become a star math instructor, for I learned from one of the deans that many students would not register for their math course if they could not have me as their instructor. Students would wait until the following semester to see if they could enroll in a course I taught.

Further, I saw students outside my class listening to me teach and later stopped to share how much they hoped I could be their instructor. I was ecstatic and happy to know I positively impacted students' desire to learn mathematics. This experience confirmed that I was exercising my God-given gift as a mathematics educator. Unfortunately, all good things ended as only two years passed when I decided to resign from Bryant & Stratton and return to MPS.

After learning of troublesome accusations from my supervisor and being placed on probation due to my class passing rates, I felt it best to leave Bryant & Stratton. The mathematics department chair was more concerned with passing students along, although they earned failing grades, rather than ensuring students thoroughly understood math. He was satisfied if instructors' course passing rates were at or above the math department's passing rate. My philosophy for teaching is that all students can learn if given the proper attention and tools. I live by this, but I could not force students to attend class, submit assignments and do well on assessments. As adults, they were responsible for putting in the work to ensure they were successful, and I would be their support system to ensure they understood the content. All I could do was encourage and motivate them to do their best and take advantage of the opportunities I provided for math help.

If students were failing my class, I did not think passing them without the knowledge necessary to advance to the next math course or graduate from their program was appropriate. Advancing students to meet a department's passing rate would disadvantage them academically and personally. I wanted students to pass because they learned the material and felt confident in their math abilities. When my supervisor said, "the number of students that failed your course translates to thousands of dollars; you are an expensive lady," I knew it was time to resign before I found myself in an unfavorable circumstance.

Additionally, during my "probation period," I was required to meet with my supervisor weekly, document every time I followed up with an absent student, and document the concepts I tutored students in at the tutoring center. These tasks were excessive and unnecessary, primarily since I was known as the math instructor many students desired to learn from on campus. Due to these extreme measures, I submitted my two weeks' notice before the start of the spring 2011 semester. My supervisor was extremely surprised as if he did not understand why I made that decision. However, I knew I was making the best choice to preserve my integrity.

Back to Basics

Returning to MPS started unpredictably because the district assigned me to a different high school, HSB. This school also served a large number of students. I was not content, although there were no significant issues or concerns. I did not feel this school was where I wanted to call home. After one semester, I decided to transfer back to HSA. Going back to HSA was a suitable resolution for the first two years. I taught math in the freshmen academy, which allowed me to nurture and prepare students well for upper-level mathematics. During this time, I was developing several math aces. Many of my students excelled in math and developed growth mindsets about learning mathematics. They began to see that there was more to math than learning inside the classroom. The concepts they explored became evident in their everyday lives, igniting excitement about learning math. These students were so accustomed to my instructional practices when they moved to higher grades, they would come back to me for help in math if they had difficulty understanding.

In addition to serving students mathematically, I was asked to design, recruit, and implement a young ladies' support group for freshmen. This venture validated my career as an educator because I was extending my area of expertise as solely a math educator. I not only had the opportunity to educate children in math, but I was able to help prepare young ladies for womanhood and college. I enjoyed working with my young ladies and teaching math until the third year at HSA began to conclude. I encountered some awful experiences with two other educators, and my position as a freshman math teacher became a weary task.

Since I taught Algebra I for five years, I realized I had become too comfortable teaching these concepts and desired to teach upper-level math courses. In addition, the behaviors of incoming freshmen began to decline, making it harder to focus on instruction. I knew I would be as successful if allowed to teach upperclassmen as I was with freshmen, especially since I had experience teaching college-level mathematics. The math content would be no problem, and my rapport with students made classroom management a breeze. Nevertheless, the principal at the time believed it was best to keep me with freshmen since I displayed excellent math content knowledge and classroom management skills, as he described it.

Further, when the unpleasant experiences with the two co-workers never came to any resolution, and my desire to advance to upper-level math courses went overlooked, I decided my time at HSA had ended. I began to think of other employment options. I found a graduate program at Marquette University for high school math teachers. I could finish my master's in math or begin a doctoral program. Since my heart was set on a master's in math, I decided to complete the master's first and then work on a doctorate.

I was accepted into the math teacher program and received a scholarship. I was enthusiastic about the chance to finally complete a master's in mathematics so I could pursue a doctorate in mathematics education. I was also pleased to have received financial support for tuition. As I proceeded through the first semester, I toiled with a math course despite trying to understand. In addition, I took simple mathematics education courses but did not earn an A as I thought I would. I felt inadequate again, especially since my grades fell below the required status to maintain the scholarship. Once more, I fled from pursuing a graduate degree in math and found out I was finally entering motherhood. Becoming a mother was an excellent excuse to take a break from school, leave HSA, and focus on me.

While I was excited about my new role as a mother and having a break from education, my life was about to change drastically. When I entered the 5th month of pregnancy, I began to experience horrible pains in my stomach that affected my ability to walk or move. I made an emergency appointment to see an Obstetrician; mine was not in the office then. I learned that my fibroids were growing due to the pregnancy, which caused the pain. Within two weeks of getting this news, I learned that my dad, Terry, had been placed in hospice with only a few days to live. He had been sick for some time; however, this situation came sooner than I had expected.

Interestingly, I had a dream approximately seven months prior that he would be dying in the coming year. Three days after hearing that he was in hospice, my daddy died. At 3:42 a.m. on July 23, 2015, his estranged wife called and said, "Telashay, he's gone," and then hung up. I gathered myself and tried to pack my suitcase while in severe pain. Within an hour, I was on 94 east heading to Michigan to prepare funeral arrangements for my daddy.

It was sad having to plan my dad's funeral with my siblings while dealing with the immense pain from my pregnancy. However, we got through it, and I knew my dad would be proud of us. I wished he had been around longer to help me welcome my little girl; he was extremely excited about me having my first child. The time between the passing of my daddy and my due date came rather quickly. I welcomed my daughter in October 2015, and six weeks later, I had to return to teaching.

The Trailblazer: My Mathematical Journey

Approximately a month before having my daughter, I selected another high school in MPS, HSC. I hoped trying a different high school would allow me to teach upper-level mathematics and get a different experience with new colleagues. Initially, I was excited when I began at HSC because I was allowed to fill in as one of the assistant principals. There were conversations about keeping me in that position, which was interesting since I had completed a leadership program at Concordia University to earn a principal and director of instruction certification. After serving in this role for six weeks, I was informed that someone else would fill the position, and I would teach math. I was assigned one Algebra II course and several freshmen-level math courses. The difference this time was the freshmen courses had a computer component that helped to support students' math abilities, and the Algebra II course had low enrollment. Although I did not have to teach much during the freshman classes, I was still unsatisfied with teaching high school.

One day I attended a workshop for high school math teachers and came across an old professor I had from the C&I department, Dr. Betty Brain. As we were catching up, I explained my desire to pursue a doctorate, and she introduced me to Dr. Steve Strick. Dr. Strick set up a meeting to discuss the urban education-mathematics education doctoral program at UWM. The program sounded like the perfect fit because I did not have to worry about math courses that may present challenges for me to pass. In addition, Dr. Strick appeared to be a supportive advisor, better than I had experienced during graduate school. I felt like my chances of getting into the program were excellent. The only hurdle I might face was earning an acceptable score on the GRE, and I was not looking forward to taking that exam. Dr. Strick assured me that if I passed the math portion and scored at least a three on the writing portion, he would admit me into the program. I put my fears aside, applied to the urban education-mathematics education program, and signed up for the GRE. God was taking great care of me because I passed the math section, earned a 3.5 on the writing portion, and was admitted into the doctoral program. I finished the semester at HSC and prepared to start graduate school to earn a doctorate.

Ph.D.: Year One

Fall 2016 arrived quickly; I was thrilled to start coursework and learn all I could on this new journey. I enrolled in Dr. Strick's Integrating Math Education Research course and Dr. Jeffrey Hawkins's Urban Education Issues course. Both of these courses were informative for different reasons. In math research, I immediately recalled how much I hated to read; funny, I know, coming from someone who had spent several years in college. We were assigned large quantities of math research articles to read, which took hours to get through and comprehend. I often felt I had not grasped the information in the articles because, during class discussions, my classmates conveyed information that never came to mind when I read. My understandings from the readings were not as in-depth as theirs. Nonetheless, I kept pushing myself to get through the articles, and by the end of the semester, I had cut down the time it took to read and felt more confident about my comprehension skills.

At the beginning of math research class, I also felt unknowledgeable about current research in mathematics. I always felt like my classmates knew more than I did and were far more advanced mathematically. I sat very quietly during lectures hoping we would not have to work in groups so others would not notice my feelings of inadequacy. Things did not work as I had hoped; we were always required to pair up and discuss articles or work on math activities. The pros to this were working with three ladies: Leah, Jenny, and Erin, who were very kind and frequently made me feel special. They loved when I asked questions or spoke about my math teaching experiences. It was as if I offered intriguing information they were uninformed about and displayed more knowledge than I realized I had.

No matter how much I tried to avoid these ladies' friendship, they showed more interest in helping me and becoming my friend. At first, I did not want to befriend them because I had become accustomed to being alone in graduate school. I was often reminded of my math department experiences of not having anyone to study with or assist me when I did not understand. As the years progressed, they proved to be the friends I needed, and they became an integral part of my journey toward completing my Ph.D.

On the contrary, Dr. Hawkins's course was very simplistic; we spent most of our classes in a Socratic seminar format. At first, I had no clue what a Socratic format was until we sat in a circle presenting information on urban education topics from our class readings. It felt like we were in a therapeutic session introducing ourselves, like, "Hi, my name is Telashay, and I am addicted to…." Boy, it took a few classes to get used to this, especially since sharing ideas was required to earn a weekly grade. Engaging in class discussions was difficult depending on the topic, as sometimes I disagreed with the majority or did not have much to say. Nonetheless, to earn my weekly grade, I had to participate. Hence, I mustered up something to say and took an unapologetic stance when sharing my thoughts.

Two of the most insightful concepts I learned in that course were 1) some white people are uninformed about situations and circumstances in black people's lives; 2) being late to Dr. Hawkins's class is a NO, NO. Expounding on the former, a white male professor ran this course, and the class consisted of predominantly white students and two black students, one of which was me. I often sat and listened to students speak of how they were unaware of the home environments of black students and how they did not know that some black students lacked access to resources that were easily accessible for white students. Furthermore, black students' home lives significantly influence their learning and performance in school. There were discussions about situations with blacks that I believed to be common knowledge, especially since the expansion of social media and the news; however, some white students expressed their unfamiliarity with such situations.

The last lesson I learned from Dr. Hawkins was that being on time was necessary, whether he was in the class or not when the clock struck 5 p.m. One night I arrived at class at 5:02 p.m. Dr. Hawkins was not present in the classroom, but he knew I was late for some reason. That one tardy affected my grade, and I was in disbelief as I was only two minutes late, so I consulted with him. He said, "it's imperative to be on time, and if you cannot, communicate that before class." I respected his position but thought at this level in graduate school and in addition to having a family and a job, there could be instances when any adult would be late unintentionally. My concern was that my grade was affected by being two minutes late, which I thought was a bit absurd.

Notwithstanding, I was never late to his class again, and two years later, when I took a second course with him, I ensured I was on time, in class before time. Dr. Hawkins earned my respect, and I grew fond of him. Dr. Hawkins later proved to be a caring professor.

Spring 2017

My first semester as a Ph.D. student went by rather quickly. I learned a few helpful lessons that prepared me for semester two. In spring 2017, I had two courses taught by professors who I would rate on opposite ends of the spectrum. Dr. Kale was on the lower end, and Dr. Bo Zhang, the higher end. I was unhappy about taking another course with Dr. Kale because of my previous experience. Yet, he was the only professor available to teach Math Program Design and Development. Luckily, Dr. Strick informed me in the fall that Dr. Kale would teach the course, so I had time to prepare mentally. Unfortunately, that mental preparation did not serve me well.

To guarantee I comprehended the course material, I talked with him privately to get his perspective on my understanding of the course. In addition, I discussed my class presentation with him to confirm if I was on the right track. Dr. Kale's feedback was, "If you believe you understand the material, you are doing well." How would such a response validate the information I should learn in the class? As for my presentation, he said, "it sounds like you're going in the right direction." Based on that conversation with Kale, I did not expect to receive a grade lower than an A, but I instead got a B. It was as if this man did not want to validate my intelligence or supposed I did not deserve to earn any grade higher than a B.

    I immediately discussed this situation with Dr. Strick, who advised me to meet with Kale. I thought Dr. Strick would have given helpful advice or volunteered to attend the meeting with me; he did not. I did not know what I would say to Kale to convince him why I should not have received a B. Past trauma resurfaced from working with Kale, making me not want to contact him. Nevertheless, I emailed him to discuss my grade, and without a response, I learned from Dr. Strick that Kale had changed my grade to an A. To this day, only God knows what happened. Did he have a change of heart? Did he change the grade so he would not have any further dealings with me? Whatever the reason, I was happy to learn I received the grade I deserved and did not have to deal with him anymore.

    Contrary to my experience with Kale, I had the pleasure of meeting Dr. Bo Zhang for Statistical Methods II. Going into this course, I was a little anxious because I had not comprehended the interpretations of the calculations performed in previous statistics courses. I instantly realized I was in good hands with Dr. Zhang. He was a kind-hearted professor who ensured his students understood all concepts covered in class. And when there were misunderstandings, he was available during class breaks, after class, and during office hours. He never made me feel inadequate, no matter how many questions I asked. After taking this course with Dr. Zhang, my confidence in statistics grew, and I developed a better understanding of interpreting statistical data. Further, I began to feel a sense of belonging as a Ph.D. student. Dr. Zhang made such an impression that I looked forward to taking more courses with him.

Summer 2017

Ending the spring semester on a high note because of Dr. Zhang, I aggressively progressed through the program and enrolled in three courses in the summer, one of which a black woman taught. I was thrilled to have a black professor and a black woman at that for the first time in my Ph.D. program. Sadly, I did not meet her in person since her course, Principles and Foundations of Adult Education, was offered online. Although I did not have the opportunity to see her physically, I was honored to be taught by someone who looked like me (same gender and race) and appreciated the knowledge she shared. I expressed my sentiments to her because it was rare to have a black professor, and it was vital for her to know how much she was valued.

The other two courses were centered on course design and gender in education. Much of what the professors presented in these courses was material I already knew; therefore, these courses did not significantly impact me. Despite this, taking three courses and teaching two courses at different institutions in different cities was a challenging balancing act. Yet, I endured and completed all tasks efficiently. I earned an A in each course while expanding my knowledge of teaching adults, designing a course, and learning about genders in an educational context.

Ph.D.: Year Two

The first year of my Ph.D. program was under my belt, and I felt good knowing that I had successfully made it through without giving up and not experiencing any personal disruptions. The great thing about this second year was that I had good professors who ensured their students learned and succeeded in their courses.

Dr. Aaron Schutz, the Urban Education program director, was one of my professors in the fall of 2017. He was an extremely patient professor and accommodating when students faced any issues. I appreciated him because he showed an interest in my education and made me feel a sense of belonging. In his Urban Education Seminar course, we were exposed to a deep analysis of critical issues in urban education while focusing on developing a literature review for a potential dissertation topic.

Dr. Aaron shared so much information with us that I always had innumerable questions. It became a joke almost every class if I did not have questions, as Dr. Aaron would say before class ended, "Telashay, are you ok? Are you sure you don't have any questions?" Or when I asked a couple of questions, and another question came to mind, it went like this: I would raise my hand and say I have a question. Dr. Aaron would say, "No, really, of course, you do; it wouldn't be normal if you didn't," and then he would laugh. My classmates and I all laughed and got right to my question. I enjoyed learning in his course, and fortunately, I had Dr. Aaron the following semester for the Advanced Seminar in Urban Education. In addition to the urban education seminar, I took a course on developing mathematics units emphasizing math standards.

Spring 2018

Spring 2018 came quickly; it felt like I sped through the fall semester. This semester, I enrolled in Survey Research Methods in Education with Dr. Zhang, Multivariate Statistics, and Advance Seminar in Urban Education. I enjoyed Dr. Zhang when I took his stats course the previous year, so I wanted to see what else I could learn statistically from him. He did not disappoint this time as I absorbed the necessary information about creating and administering surveys for research and how to prepare a poster presentation for research conferences. I was so impressed with Dr. Zhang that I had to have him on my dissertation committee. When I asked if he would be a member, without hesitation, he said yes. I was overjoyed and anticipated what else I could learn from working more closely with him.

Since my confidence in statistics increased, I decided to take another statistics course. I chose Multivariate Statistics for a mathematical and statistical challenge, especially since we were not required to take regular mathematics courses. I was a bit nervous but gained the courage to enroll. This course had challenging aspects: learning to use statistical analysis software (SAS) and studying for tests. Dr. Zhang introduced me to SAS in his class; however, we also learned how to use the statistical package for the social sciences (SPSS) software which was more straightforward. SAS required one to input data and then enter commands to run tests, whereas, with SPSS, one only had to enter data and choose the necessary test to run.

Studying for tests produced anxiety because we had to use SAS to analyze data. If one minor mistake occurred entering the commands, the software would not run to produce the result. I struggled to determine errors made while inputting commands, resulting in extra time to complete homework and prepare for tests. In preparation for in-class tests, I studied with Leah to ensure I could input my commands successfully. Surprisingly, I did well in the course, expanded my knowledge of analyzing and interpreting data, and earned an A-. I was pleased about this.

Angel in Disguise

The last and most crucial professor I met in the Spring of 2018 was Dr. Elizabeth "Liz" Drame. Dr. Liz is a Black professor who teaches special education courses. I was referred to her by Dr. Strick because of my interest in studying abroad. She was a Fulbright scholar and had expertise about the Fulbright scholarship program. Dr. Liz was excited to meet with me to share information about applying for the Fulbright scholarship. She explained that conducting research as part of a study abroad experience could extend my graduation timeline. After I explained my research topic and knew that I desired to graduate within two years, I changed my mind about studying abroad. I did not know at that moment how lucky I was to have at least met Dr. Liz. Katherine Johnson said, "luck is a combination of preparation and opportunity. If you're prepared and the opportunity comes up, it's your good fortune to have been in the right place at the right time." Meeting Dr. Liz that day was perfect timing for several reasons. She informed me of information about studying abroad that gave me insight into how that opportunity works. I was walking into a blessing I did not realize I needed.

After discussing my research topic with Dr. Liz, she became intrigued and offered to be my second dissertation committee member. I was ecstatic and could not believe that a meeting with her would become an opportunity for her to join my committee. Dr. Liz became very fond of me, and the feelings were mutual. I quickly learned how indispensable she would be in obtaining my Ph.D. She assuredly was an angel in disguise.

Ph.D.: Year Three

As my coursework ended, I began to feel a sense of accomplishment. I took one course over the summer, leaving one remaining for fall 2018 and my preliminary exam. My last course was with Dr. Hawkins for Qualitative Research Field Study. In this course, Dr. Hawkins displayed personality traits I did not realize he had during the urban education issues course. He was unique, for his personality was like no other-funny, semi-strict and sympathetic. His ability to sympathize with me became more evident during this class.

In this course, he exposed us to various research journals and the process of preparing research proposals for the American Educational Research Association (AERA). According to Dr. Hawkins, by this time in the program, students should have at least had conversations with their advisor about co-authoring opportunities on research projects and preparing to submit proposals to their subject area research journals. To our surprise, Dr. Strick had not offered any such opportunities for me. Therefore, Dr. Hawkins ensured I understood the process for preparing and submitting proposals to AERA. I was grateful for his concern and assistance, which later paid off when I was invited to present my dissertation at a round table research discussion through AERA for graduate students.

My second task for the fall 2018 semester was to complete my preliminary exam. This exam is defended in front of a student's dissertation committee. My dissertation committee consisted of Dr. Strick, Dr. Zhang, Dr. Liz, and Dr. Leigh Van de Kieboom. Dr. Leigh was the last member who graciously joined, although she was a professor at Marquette University and had never met me. Her expertise was in elementary mathematics education, which was helpful since my dissertation topic was related to elementary teachers.

The mathematics education specialization preliminary exam consisted of three questions associated with math education, urban education, and research methods; we had two weeks to complete these questions. The responses to these questions had to be supported by current research conducted within the last twenty years. I was happy with our time frame but was overtaken with anxiety when it was time to defend my responses in front of my committee. I did not know what to expect during the prelim defense as I was not given any details or instructions for what would take place besides speaking about my responses to the questions.

On the day of my defense, I entered the room with my laptop and typed responses, then stood before my committee with no understanding of what would happen next. I wondered if this process would be informal, like a presentation where I could refer to my responses if needed. Would it be like an assessment where notes are prohibited? Should I stand before my committee at the podium as if I were reciting a speech? Or sit at the table with them as if we were conversing? Was I to start the session by welcoming and thanking everyone for being there? I felt like a lost cause.

I finally got up enough courage to ask my advisor what the expectations were. He attended the meeting virtually and had not given me insight into the protocol. He said, "I'll start by explaining how the defense will go. You will stand and summarize your responses, answer questions posed by the committee, and then step out of the room to allow the committee to deliberate about your performance." The time had come to carry out those procedures, and the anxiety never left my body. I summarized my responses, and the questions began to roll in. As committee members threw questions at me, one after another, my confidence sank to the floor as it appeared that I was not comprehending what they were asking me. It felt like I was struggling to provide adequate responses to their questions.

The next thing I knew, my angel slid her copy of my prelim responses in front of me and said, "refer to them if you need to." At that point, I did not feel a need to refer to them because I wasn't sure if they would be any help. She then spoke up and said she would keep track of feedback provided by all committee members. I felt a slight sense of relief but left the room feeling defeated. My mind became filled with numerous questions: Why didn't Dr. Strick prepare me for this defense? Why didn't he speak up for me, refer me to my notes, or offer to keep track of committee members' feedback? Is this how prelim defenses usually go? What happens if I fail? As I tried to refocus my thoughts, I stood in front of a window looking across campus, thinking I had come to the end of my educational journey. If I had failed, I didn't know my next step. Would I get a second attempt at the defense? Would I be dismissed from the program? If I was dismissed, what would I do, go back to teaching high school math? Feeling sad and let down, I heard Dr. Liz calling my name as she came out to look for me. She had a slight smile, but that did not indicate how I fared because Dr. Liz always wore a warm, sweet smile.

After returning to the room, Dr. Strick delivered the verdict. "Congratulations Telashay; you passed your preliminary defense with revisions." He explained that although I had revisions for one question, they were impressed with the thought I put into my responses. Dr. Liz agreed as past experiences with some of her advisees showed minimal thought-provoking responses. I was left with mixed emotions—unpreparedness and happiness because I performed better than expected. Finishing my prelims began a new and unpleasant experience with Dr. Strick.

Disintegration

I was happy I passed my prelims and felt good that I only had to revise one question. Dr. Strick said he would advise me on current literature to support my responses. I was finally getting his assistance with this process, which increased my confidence until we had our first uncomfortable experience.

I found new articles and emailed them to him to get his approval and prepare for revisions. I wanted to ensure I met the two-week deadline he issued. I emailed him on a Monday; I remember this incident like yesterday. Two days passed, and I had not received a response. With two days left to meet my deadline, I wanted to be sure he received my email just in case it did not go through. Therefore, I sent a follow-up email that Wednesday, then he finally replied. His message stated, "I have received it, and I will respond when I have an opportunity to do so. That time is not now." Oh my, did the end of that message sound as if he was annoyed; it was unprofessional. That made me uncomfortable and left the impression that it was not good to follow up with him. This incident made me timid when emailing him and following up with other professors. From that day forward, I always felt apprehensive about emailing him. That situation was strike one with Dr. Strick; little did I know more strikes were forthcoming.

After finishing my prelims, I learned that my status as a student should change from graduate student to dissertator. Dissertator status occurs when a student has completed all coursework and passed the preliminary exam. I needed to complete a form and get Dr. Strick's approval to move to this status. One might think he would have had this conversation with me after finishing my prelims or even before, but he did not. The graduate school required the completed form at the beginning of the semester following the preliminary exam. Due to my last communication with Dr. Strick, I was leery about contacting him for approval. However, I contacted him, everything worked out, and I began the spring 2019 semester as a dissertator.

Spring 2019

As I mentally prepared for the spring semester, Dr. Strick aimlessly informed me that my dissertation topic was changing. I was unhappy since I had started compiling my literature review and research methods ideas in previous courses. Dr. Strick said my dissertation topic should evolve from my preliminary exam questions. I immediately felt clueless because he had never informed me about the process of determining a dissertation topic. I thought I would proceed with what I had begun researching in previous courses.

Dr. Strick had a different view, and being my advisor and committee chair, I had to go along with his vision and change most of the work I had completed. I now sensed a setback because I had to decide how my prelim responses could inform my new topic, then collect new articles, read them, and synthesize them to formulate a new literature review. If there was anything positive from this, I was familiar with the work I'd completed for my prelims and had experience writing a literature review from my courses.

I spent the month of January searching for additional articles and books to familiarize myself with my new dissertation topic. This search entailed many hours of reading, determining how meaningful this new topic would be for potential readers and me. Sunday, February 3rd, arrived, and I had a ton of articles collected and ready to be printed so I could begin reading and synthesizing these authors' views about my topic. One might wonder how I could remember this exact day; here is how.

Sunday, February 3rd, was Super Bowl Sunday. My biological father, Rodney, called that morning to check on me before leaving for church. We chatted for a few minutes, and later that evening, I called him to see what he had cooked. He loved cooking and watching sports, so I knew he had been in the kitchen. He told me all the food he had prepared and that his dessert would be cheesecake purchased by my sister, Joia. We laughed about his meal, and I let him go. After that call, I began to think of how unusual it had been for my father to call on Sunday mornings; he had called the past few Sundays. He always began the conversation with "hey, daughter" and ended with, "love you, daughter." I knew my dad loved me, but this consistent pattern was different. I had no clue that my new and frequent Sunday morning calls were about to end.

Desensitized

Monday, February 4th, 2019, I was heading to work around 7 a.m. when I received a call from my sister Joia. It was peculiar to get a call from her early in the morning, but I did not panic. I thought maybe my dad was not feeling well; he was on dialysis and had syncope. Yet, when I answered the phone, my sister said, "Tee, daddy is gone." I was like, huh, what do you mean? She said, "daddy died this morning on his way to dialysis." I was in shock and at a loss for words, but I held it together as I continued driving into the parking garage. As the oldest child and big sister, I did not want to make her sadder than she was, so I tried my best not to cry. After notifying my supervisor and students about my dad, I canceled my class for the day, went straight home, packed clothes, and headed for Michigan. On my way to Michigan, I emailed Dr. Strick to inform him of my father's passing and that I would try to get some work done while preparing for the funeral. He responded two days later, "I'm sorry to hear that. Thanks for letting me know. Safe travels." Not much more than that.

     I planned my father's funeral in three days and had the funeral Saturday, February 9th. I sat at the funeral desensitized; I did not feel a thing and could not think or process what was happening. I could hear the music and the pastor speaking, but everything was a blur. I returned to Milwaukee that Monday and could not complete schoolwork for two months. In my downtime while in Michigan, I thought I would be able to read or at least do so when I returned home, but I could not think or put myself up to doing much of anything.

Comeback

     After two months of stillness and accomplishing nothing academically or personally, I knew I had to return to schoolwork. I did not want to jeopardize my chances of graduating the following year. Thus, I thought the best plan would be to meet with Dr. Liz to get insight into the steps following my literature review. I could have contacted Dr. Strick, but Dr. Liz came to mind first. I presumed I would get more clarity to get back on track with her assistance. Meeting with Dr. Liz was always refreshing; she gave great advice and never made me uncomfortable or left me uninformed. Dr. Liz invariably ensured I felt confident about the doctoral process and my work and gave great tips for keeping track of the information we discussed. For example, she would often say when we started our meetings, "hey, you're not recording," I would laugh and grab my phone immediately. When we met, I was comfortable and focused, and my mind was at ease. I was fixed on consuming information while maximizing her time, thus forgetting to record our sessions. Recording our conversations was extremely helpful because the doctoral process entails a tremendous amount of information and has various stages.

During that meeting, we discussed the order of tackling the chapters of my dissertation. Chapter one is the introduction; chapter two is the literature review; chapter three is the methodology; chapter four is the analysis; and chapter five is the conclusion. Dr. Liz believed preparing the methodology chapter first, the literature review second, and the introduction last would be a good plan since the introduction and literature review are easier to compile. Additionally, the methods chapter dictates the success of the analysis and conclusion chapters. Dr. Liz also advised me to meet with Dr. Zhang to determine a research method I could use for my new topic since he was the committee expert for the methods chapter of my dissertation. My new topic was math anxiety (MA), mathematics teaching anxiety (MTA), and its impact on in-service elementary teachers' mathematics instruction. When choosing a research method, one can select quantitative, qualitative, or mixed methods (quantitative and qualitative).

Next, I met with Dr. Zhang to determine the best approach for choosing my research methods. Initially, he was concerned about me jumping back into my work so soon after my father's death; however, I assured him I was ready and needed to get back on track. My mind was fixated on finishing school to have an ordinary life again. Dr. Zhang and I discussed how MA and MTA could interact and influence elementary teachers' math instruction. We discussed a visual model that would be sensible for connecting these constructs. After our meeting, I was more assured about writing chapter three.

Now that I had met with two committee members, I was recharged and ready to work on the first three chapters of my dissertation. I contacted Dr. Strick to schedule a potential proposal defense date since that task consisted of defending the first three chapters. Passing the proposal defense shows that a student has a well-thought-out plan for researching their dissertation topic and the topic has academic merit. Dr. Strick was on board with my plan and asked that I submit these chapters to him for review at the beginning of August.

Summer 2019

I spent the summer working on chapter three, determining how to use a mixed methods approach to best research my topic. Since I knew I would have several revisions to all chapters, I could save time by writing chapter three using past tense language. I did not think this idea would raise any red flags with my committee members because everyone should have known that I was not at the point of collecting any data for the analysis. However, after completing chapter three and submitting it to Dr. Strick, he assumed I had skipped all protocols and jumped into data collection. To collect data, a student must have their first three chapters approved by their advisor, pass the proposal defense, then apply to the institutional review board (IRB) for approval to work with human subjects (targeted population of people). There was no way I had completed these steps, and Dr. Strick knew this because I never submitted all three chapters to him or completed the proposal defense.

Yet, after reading chapter three, Dr. Strick contacted me for a phone conversation. He spoke to me intensely, accusing me of moving forward with data collection without going through the proper channels. He explained that he would need to contact the IRB and inform them that I had bypassed their requirements and begun recruiting participants for my study. My heart immediately sank to my stomach, and fear took over my entire body because I knew I had not broken any rules, and I was unsure of the result of his accusations. Yes, I had a potential school district and targeted participants in mind, but I had not spoken to anyone. The only step I took was to meet with the research coordinator at UWM since she was the point of contact for that school district. We only discussed the recruitment process; thus, I had not defied any IRB guidelines.

Dr. Strick did not believe me because he explained he would conduct an investigation to see if I was being truthful, and I would need to cease all work I was performing until I heard back from him. When that conversation concluded, I felt our trust was broken, and he was convinced I was incompetent in adhering to the required regulations. How he spoke to me on the phone made me feel incapable and dishonest. I was in tears after hanging up and considered this incident strike two. My comfort level and faith in Dr. Strick as an advisor diminished even more, and the rest of my day was ruined.

I couldn't think clearly and was hesitant about what to do next. I was out of town at a church convention, studying in a room when this event occurred. I sat still while my heart pounded, wondering what was going through Strick's mind and what would happen next. I collected myself and then called Dr. Liz for advice.

I trusted she would guide me on what I should do or what might occur as I waited to hear from Dr. Strick. She assured me everything would be fine as I had not done anything wrong, and this situation was a big misunderstanding. However, she explained that writing using past tense language was not a good idea until I had completed the data collection process. Further, I should write in the present tense, although I would have to go back and change to the past tense for the final dissertation. A big lesson learned — working smarter, not harder, is not always the best approach.

After some days, Dr. Strick realized I had not collected data without IRB approval. He never apologized for the accusations or discussed the situation. Strick permitted me to proceed with chapters one and two, so I could set a proposal defense date. I submitted chapters 1–3 to Strick on August 1st, and within a week, he informed me that I was not ready for my proposal defense. He disagreed with the direction of my dissertation topic and methodological approach. I was like, here we go again, another delay. I wondered if we could reschedule the defense date for September since professors were extremely busy, and it could be challenging to pick a feasible date for all committee members. Of course, Strick did not agree and suggested I focus on my topic first.

Ph.D.: Year Four

The fall semester of 2019 began very shaky. Strick and I could not seem to get in one accord regarding the direction of my research. I'd do everything he asked me to, but then he would find an issue with something else. It was as if he was speaking a language I could not grasp, and his guidance became vastly abstract and unobtainable. I had minimal clarity and felt like I was spinning my wheels while running out of time to achieve a proposal defense date. In addition, I sensed his tolerance for me had decreased, and it felt like he did not want to advise me any longer. These feelings became evident as the next couple of events unfolded.

Strick was away from the university working for an agency that followed eastern standard time; we use central standard time in Milwaukee. While I knew he was away, he never informed me of his exact location; therefore, I had no clue we were in different time zones. We had a phone meeting one day, and I was late due to the time zone difference. I received an email from him asking if we were meeting that day or not. I instantly panicked and ran to call him, only to be received with what appeared to be an attitude. I apologized for the mix-up, and his response was, "I don't have much time remaining, so it's best to reschedule." I understood my mistake but did not appreciate his lack of understanding and tone.

Once again, I consulted Dr. Liz about my experience and desired to change advisors, for I no longer felt comfortable working with him. I believed I was not progressing. I was unsure if he thought I no longer had the potential to succeed. Was I not measuring up to the type of student he was used to advising? Did he feel I was a different student now than I was when he first admitted me into the program? All these thoughts flooded my mind, but Dr. Liz encouraged me not to give up and hang in there. She explained that it is not ideal to change advisors and that doing so could have repercussions. I took her advice and tried to ignore my reservations about Strick.

Not much time passed when the final straw occurred. Since our meetings took place on the phone, I used a recording app, Tape-A-Call, so it would be easier to keep track of the information we discussed. Strick and I had a meeting to discuss work that needed his approval. I emailed the work before our meeting, yet again, he did not confirm receipt of receiving the work. Past occurrences prevented me from following up with him. Instead, I prayed to get myself in a positive head space as I never knew what type of mood he might be in.

I started the call optimistically by greeting him and asking how he was doing. He was short with me, but I did not allow that to be a distraction. I asked if he had received my work, and he replied I did not. I told him I had emailed it a few days prior so he would have time to review it and prepare for our meeting. He said, "again, I do not have it" then there was silence for almost a minute. During this time, I thought maybe he was double-checking his email. When the silence continued to linger, I asked if he could find it, and he replied with a loud, disrespectful tone, "I said I don't have it, and I said it several times." I felt my heart drop again, but this time it was worse; it felt like my breath had left my body. I did not know how to proceed with the conversation.

Nonetheless, I searched for the document, resent it, and informed him I did. I felt violated and knew this would be my last meeting with Strick. I no longer saw a future with him as an advisor and had to find a way out of this partnership. Like clockwork, I scheduled an in-person conference with Dr. Liz to share that encounter. This time, I had proof. I wanted her thoughts to see if I was overreacting or if what I experienced was real. After listening to the recording, she validated my feelings. She advised me to schedule a meeting with the program director, Dr. Aaron, to present my case and determine if changing advisors was an option. She volunteered to become my advisor if Dr. Aaron approved since she was not math faculty.

Traditionally an advisor is in the same subject area as the student.

I contacted Dr. Aaron, and he agreed to meet with me. After I explained all the issues that had taken place and allowed him to hear the recording, he also agreed that it would be in my best interest to switch advisors. Dr. Aaron sympathized with me and affirmed that I was not taking these events personally; they were valid, and my emotions and feelings were real. He approved of Dr. Liz taking over as my advisor and even offered to become my advisor or sit on my committee. I was honored and appreciated by his offer. Knowing that two professors had compassion for me and wanted to ensure I succeeded proved that I belonged in the urban education-math education program and could thrive.

Dr. Liz devoting herself to being my advisor showed that she empathized with me as she had an abnormal experience with her advisor while obtaining her Ph.D. She did not receive appropriate guidance from him, leaving her to figure out many things independently. She frequently counseled me about Strick and often reflected on her experiences. My journey with Strick ignited a spark within her to take me under her wing and provide the guidance, support, and resources I needed to pick up the pieces and get back on track. She had my best interest at heart, and my fondness for her grew considerably. Her first priority as my committee chair (advisor) was to find a new committee member to replace her current role. She introduced me to Dr. Sara Jozwik, an associate professor skilled in literacy development. Dr. Sara quickly became an asset to my committee, and I was ready to move forward.

With all the changes that transpired that semester, there was no time to plan for my proposal defense. Dr. Liz explained this in a caring way but assured me that if I put in the work to reset and refocus on the ideas I was currently formulating, I could potentially be ready for a proposal defense in February 2020. She was great with backward planning, so we set dates to accomplish specific tasks, then designed a timeline to reach the desired goals. I had faith in her as she was the brains behind my initial plan of completing chapters 1-3 in three months to prepare for the first proposal defense date.

Dr. Liz's second priority was for me to reconsider the introduction chapter. I needed to reorganize my thoughts, reposition information, and shine a light on who I was as a mathematics researcher with experience teaching students of color. She explained the importance of positionality in research and how I had not conveyed my position as a black woman researcher. Positionality is how one communicates their race, gender, class, etc., in their research, identifying how those constructs influence and potentially bias one's understanding of the information presented. It was significant for me to identify as a black woman in mathematics, a white male-dominated field, with experience teaching a diverse population of students in urban settings. My teaching experience gave me insight into students' struggles while learning math. Thus, biases could have developed around research participants' math instructional techniques. With Dr. Liz's direction, I was back on track, had confidence again, and was ready to progress on my dissertation.

Spring 2020: Energized

A trip out of the country was an excellent way to reset and re-energize. I had always dreamed of visiting Africa and was blessed to travel to Ghana, West Africa, for two and a half weeks in January. This trip was organized and offered through my employer Milwaukee Area Technical College. The purpose of this study abroad trip was cultural immersion and self-discovery, which I enjoyed through three different experiences: residing with my host family and visiting famous tourist sites and schools.

Living in Ghana

Living with a host family allows one to explore what it is like to live and eat in Ghana. Residing with Ghanaians was very interesting for several reasons. First, I enjoyed African cuisine for breakfast and dinner most days. African breakfast consists of much lighter options than what we enjoy in America. My choices were boiled eggs, toast, fresh smoothies, coffee, milo (breakfast drink), and water. There were four selections of smoothies: purple delight (as my host-mom called it) made from mango and beetroot; an orange-colored one made with pineapple, banana, and coconut; a green one made with avocado, banana, and honey; and a red one. Having a gluten allergy, I could not have toast, and I did not prefer boiled eggs daily, so my host mom, Mrs. Veronica, made plain oatmeal for me. Although I appreciated having other options, I wanted a different flavor. Thus I started crumbling nature's valley peanut butter granola into the oatmeal to give it a spin; it tasted delicious.

Dinner was more exciting and enjoyable. My first dinner was Red Red—black-eyed peas made with palm oil, rice, and fried plantains. I was so sick from the plane ride that I could not enjoy my dinner as much as I would have liked. Nonetheless, it was delicious and memorable; it was the only dish I attempted to cook when I returned home. In addition to the Red Red, I enjoyed Mrs. Veronica's white fish, sauteed potatoes, and mixed vegetables.

Each day we had lunch at various restaurants while exploring Ghana. I rarely ate lunch because most African dishes were spicy; I do not prefer spicy foods. While dining at one restaurant, I thought I could enjoy a bowl of mushroom soup, one of my favorites. However, to my surprise, it was also spicy. I was highly annoyed, which resulted in eating French fries instead. Eating in Ghana was not enjoyable unless I ate dinner prepared by my host mother. I lost five pounds while in Ghana, and it was evident I had not eaten much.

The second intriguing aspect of living with a host family was washing clothes. I was not accustomed to their washer machine, and there was no dryer. The washer was a small square unit that sat in the shower and had to be filled with water and drained. It had a few settings that appeared simple to understand; however, none worked when I turned the machine on. The cleaning cycle never seemed to work, and the water never drained during the rinse cycle. I was clueless and thought, I'll have to deal with half-cleaned clothes for a few days. Not on Mrs. Veronica's watch. When I told her of my inexperience using her washer, she had her house helper wash my clothes. Clothes were dried on a clothesline outside. Line-drying clothes outside reminded me of how my Nana used to dry specific clothing and bed sheets when I was younger. Being without a washer and dryer was one of my humbling experiences in Ghana. It made me appreciate the access to and procession of luxuries we sometimes take for granted in America.

The last memorable part of living with my host family was taking showers. The bathroom in our living quarters was tiny and consisted of a sink and walk-in shower; the toilet was in a separate room next door. The walk-in shower was small, with a hand-held shower head. The water pressure was low, and there was no hot water. The good thing was most days, the weather was scorching hot, and their heat was more humid than ours. Thus, having a cold shower helped cool me down during the night before bed since we did not have air conditioning, only a ceiling fan.

Her home was pleasant and divided into at least three living quarters. She and her husband lived in one area; her two sons lived in a second area above theirs, and a third area accommodated the house help and students studying abroad. Mrs. Veronica's family was welcoming. Her family consisted of her husband, two sons, a daughter, two granddaughters, and one dog.

Living with a host family was an enjoyable experience because I had first-hand knowledge of Ghanaians' everyday life. Mrs. Veronica willingly engaged in meaningful conversations about her family, life in Accra, African cuisine, and African attire. She was even nice enough to take my measurements to have a beautiful white two-piece dress made for my mother.

Tourist Attractions

My host family and personal tour guide taught me a lot about Ghana's rich history. Our tour guide played a significant role when visiting several tourist attractions. The most memorable attractions were Elmina and Cape Coast—two cities that housed slave castles, and Mfantsiman — a municipality that contained Krofu Village. Kumasi, Kwame Nkrumah Memorial Park, and the W.E.B Dubois Museum were also informative tourist attractions we explored.

Exploring the slave castles in Elmina and Cape Coast was very emotional. Standing on the floors where many enslaved people laid, defecated, urinated, and vomited was a sight. After all these years, the red brick floors are still covered with enslaved people's bodily fluids. Walking through the male and female dungeons with little air flow brought tears to my eyes and evoked mixed emotions. Knowing that enslaved people were thrown in cells without ventilation was disheartening.

Enslaved women were chained to weights and not fed for refusing to have intercourse with generals, and dead bodies were thrown into the ocean as if they were seafood. A rage of anger began bubbling inside me as I listened to the castle tour guide while feeling the spirits of the enslaved people around me. I stood still on the rooftop of one of the castles listening to the tour guide speak of how enslaved people were taken out to the ocean in chains to board slave boats; I could not imagine life during that time Although I was thankful for hearing firsthand from Africans how enslaved people were mistreated being in the midst of that environment saddened me. I was honored to be there and pay my respects and sympathy for the thousands of innocent lives taken from this earth for reasons of power and authority. Yet, I took frequent walks away from the group to collect myself and renew my mind so I would not explode with a cry of sorrow.

    A visit to the slave castles is one experience that every human being, especially blacks, should undertake. I believe participating in such an experience will forever impact an individual's life. It indeed developed a deeper appreciation for my ancestors and what it means to identify as Black. Black means strength, integrity, sacrifice, and bravery. When I think back to the slave castles, I'm reminded of the song:

"I am Free, Praise the Lord, I'm Free. No longer bound, no more chains holding me. My soul is resting, it's such a blessing. Praise the Lord, Hallelujah. I'm free."

A second emotional experience occurred when I visited Krofu village in Mfantsiman to take school supplies to students. Krofu is a small village made up of one family. As the van drove into the village and came to a stop, I gazed at a group of small children standing outside and the small buildings that made up their school area. I began to sob as if grieving over a

deceased loved one. I couldn't gather my emotions or tears as we were instructed to leave the van. I was so emotional that some trip participants wondered what was wrong with me and if I would be ok. I could barely speak to explain what I was feeling at that moment.

As I stepped out of the van and walked closer to the children, I was able to articulate my emotions as a deep sense of humility and happiness to see the high spirits of the children laughing and playing outside. The children's big smiles spoke of happiness, contentment, and enjoyment. Looking at them in this state was a bit strange, seeing their living conditions.

In the village, there was a lack of restrooms;they used an outhouse that did not contain toilet paper or running water to wash their hands. There were no air conditioners, unsealed windows, or cafeterias inside the school buildings.

The children appeared oblivious to living in these conditions. There I was with unlimited access to all these essentials, complaining about restrooms we had access to, paying to use a public restroom, not having much to eat, and other simplistic things while I was there. How silly I felt at that moment. God brought Philippians 2:14 to my mind, "do all things without complaining and disputing," and 1 Thessalonians 5:18, "in everything give thanks; for this is the will of God in Christ Jesus for you" (NASB).

After gathering myself, I walked over to an area where two women cooked lunch for the students. I could not determine what they were preparing, but I noticed their happiness and joy in caring for the students. Their work and dedication inspired me; hence I gave them cedis (Ghanaian money) to help purchase food for the students. Next, the schoolmaster led me into the first school building that housed younger-aged students. Those babies were so excited they quickly ran into the building and piled into seats,

two or three students on each bench as if I were their teacher or a celebrity. The students could tell I was a visitor; of course, I looked different from them, but also because they began to showcase their knowledge by singing and reciting information as if to make an impression. I was so impressed that I forgot that I was supposed to be with the junior high students. The schoolmaster signaled for me to leave that building to go to the building for the upper-class students.

Before entering the junior high class, there was a request for me to teach the students' math concepts. What in the world, I disclaimed? Where did that request come from? What would I show them? Nonetheless, I honored the request and considered a few basic algebraic concepts. As I entered the class, the students stood up and greeted me, "Good morning, Madam," and Lord have mercy on me; the tears started flowing again. I was impressed and humbled by their respect for me, a stranger. Their greeting was an action I was not used to as an educator in the US. I calmed myself to begin teaching and quickly saw the students' intelligence. I switched gears by asking them what they preferred to learn to avoid wasting time on concepts they already knew.

The students and I enjoyed each other so much that their teacher did not want me to leave. I learned that students in junior high study math by subject rather than grade level. Therefore, the junior high class consisted of students of various ages. In addition, these students are not allowed to use calculators. They are expected to learn and understand math concepts without electronic devices because math concepts in junior high are considered simple and easy to complete mentally.

In addition to learning how classes are organized, I learned the importance of respect and honor from a Ghanaian perspective. Respect and honor are of top priority in African villages; therefore, before we could visit the children, we had to go and speak with the village chief first. It is tradition for the village elders to be present when speaking with the village chief. Thus, we had to wait for the schoolmaster to assemble a few elders so the chief could come in to see us. Once the chief and elders came in and sat down, the trip director gave the chief a gift. When someone visits the chief, it is customary to bring a present. Hence, our trip director purchased bottles of beer from a vendor in the village so we would not go before the chief emptied-handed. The beer had to be presented first before explaining the reason for our visit.

The trip director explained who we were and the purpose of our tour—to provide school supplies and books for the students. The chief approved and granted blessings upon us. He was kind enough to take pictures with us and extended his gratitude for our thoughtfulness and visit. Spending time at Krofu village was another humbling experience, an exploration that I'll cherish forever.

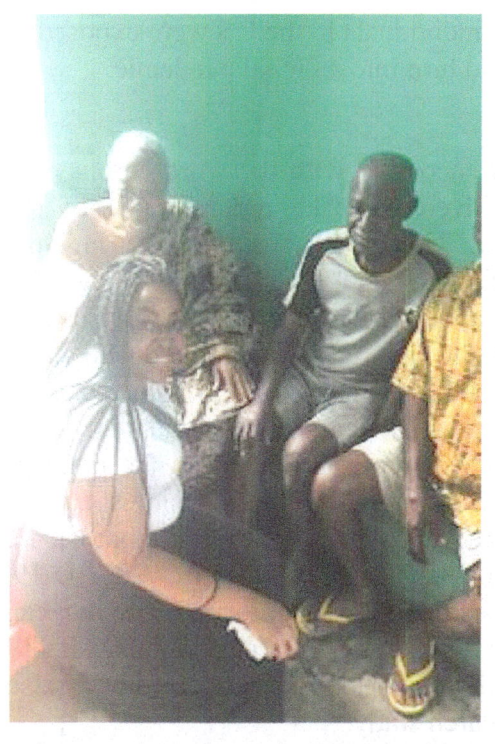

My trip to Ghana was vital because it took place during a transformative time of my Ph.D. experience. The trip fueled my passion and drive to educate students in mathematics and to travel to other countries. I learned how people are generally educated about life skills in Ghana, how students learn in school, and how knowledgeable Africans are about their history. My appreciation for obtaining an education and pursuing a doctorate was enriched.

COVID-19 Pandemic

Imagine being at a place that brings you a great deal of joy. You are in your element, having the time of your life, so much so that you have no clue what is happening around you. I had this sort of experience while studying abroad in Ghana. When I returned home after being there for half of January, I had no clue that individuals in the US were exposed to a virus that would turn into a global pandemic.

My first encounter with the word coronavirus was when I delivered a cake order to one of my business clients. He asked, "did you bring the coronavirus back with you?" I said, corona-what, what are you talking about? I had no clue that a virus had begun to affect the lives of many individuals. Little did I know that two months later, in March 2020, we would be entering a pandemic that would shut down our economy and disrupt our society to the point of having to stay home with limited business access. After being on lockdown for several months, we began hearing about the new term COVID-19. COVID-19 is a contagious respiratory disease that can cause severe illness or death. Not only did COVID-19 cause many individuals to stay indoors, but it also affected my research study.

I passed my proposal defense in February and could apply for IRB approval to start data collection. The proposal defense consisted of presenting the dissertation's first three chapters and anticipated results from data collection in a summarized form. During my proposal defense, I was nervous about my performance and if my committee would agree with the direction of my study. I recalled my experience during my prelim defense. However, I executed my proposal defense well and believed I did because Dr. Liz explained the expectations and allowed me to submit my presentation to her in advance for feedback. She set me up for success, which is what advisors should do so that their students progress effectively through the program. I now had the green light to apply for IRB approval. The IRB process consisted of completing a form detailing eight aspects of the dissertation. A few of these facets are a summary highlighting the significance and purpose of the study, the targeted research population, study activities, and the benefits and risks of participation in the study.

The IRB must review research studies that involve human subjects to determine the level of risk to participants. There are three review levels:
Level 1 — If there is no greater than minimal risk to participants or no participants are part of a study; the study can be exempt from review.
Level 2 — An expedited review is conducted if there is minimal risk, as ordinarily typical in daily life.
Level 3 — A full review occurs when a study involves a vulnerable population of participants (children, prisoners, elderly, disadvantaged persons, etc.).
These descriptions are a concise overview as the levels of review are more in-depth than what I explained. My study was in evaluation for approximately two weeks and qualified for expedited review. This time frame was relatively quick, and I had a few corrections to make.

I was excited to contact my targeted school district to begin data collection. However, due to the COVID-19 pandemic, some schools closed for the remainder of the school year, some transitioned to virtual learning, and others used alternative means for educating students. With all this happening, I was unsure if I could collect data. I was disappointed because that meant graduation and data collection would be delayed; however, I understood the severity of the pandemic. I was reminded of the phrase, delayed, not denied. This circumstance provided an opportunity to enhance my research topic again.

Since my research topic was related to instruction, Dr. Liz suggested I take advantage of virtual learning and incorporate this new teaching method into my study if schools did not return to in-person learning in the fall. At this time, many educational stakeholders hoped to use the summer to plan methods for getting students back into the buildings for learning in the fall. However, there was a lot of uncertainty about the COVID-19 pandemic.

I was also in doubt about my process for data collection for the fall semester. Would principals still be interested in allowing me to observe teachers in person?; Would teachers agree to participate?; Would I collect enough data to conduct a valid study? All of these questions filled my mind. Even so, I had to devise a plan that would allow me to keep progressing toward graduation. I returned to the drawing board and revised chapters one and two to incorporate research on virtual learning and COVID-19. I earnestly prayed that some targeted schools would agree to participate in my study. I mentally prepared myself to collect data using any method in case I could not enter school buildings in the fall.

Ph.D.: Year Five

My final fall semester of school came. I was excited to begin recruiting participants for my research study. In the beginning, I targeted a school district consisting of ten schools. However, only two schools were willing to participate due to the pandemic. Once I spoke with the principals of these two schools, nine prospective teachers were available to recruit. After several attempts to gain all nine teachers, only two completed all recruitment materials and remained dedicated to my research study. Theoretically, two teachers would not suffice for the design of my study; therefore, I decided to restructure my research to a case study. By choosing this option, I would not have to prolong my current timeline by attempting to target more schools to gain more participants.

Changing to a case study meant adding more information to my topic. Nevertheless, I had two teachers willing to participate, and I did not want to lose them or extend my graduation timeline, attempting to recruit more teachers. When a researcher tries recruiting participants for a study, one never knows how that process might conclude. Thus, it was best to stick with the two teachers I had and spend a little time learning about case study research.

Data Collection

Collecting data was exciting and probably the most fun of preparing my dissertation. I asked participants to complete two surveys: math anxiety and math teaching self-efficacy. Based on these surveys, I could identify their math anxiety level and belief in their ability to teach mathematics effectively. Teachers were then interviewed about their mathematics instruction and observed by me three times while teaching math. Last, a post-observation interview took place to follow up with any questions I had regarding my observations of their teaching. Once I collected all of this information, I analyzed it to look for themes that helped me understand how math anxiety and math teaching self-efficacy influenced elementary teachers' virtual math instruction.

I learned from data collection that there are questions and information that a researcher may not have thought about when preparing surveys, interview questions, and research instruments. Post-observation interviews can be helpful in this situation. Still, the post-observation questions are predetermined and may not capture every possible nuance of the topic. Yet, a researcher must make conclusions based on the information collected.

Spring 2021

"For the vision is yet for the appointed time; It hurries toward the goal and it will not fail. Though it delays, wait for it; For it will certainly come, it will not delay long" Habakkuk 2:3 (NASB).

Although I faced many challenges completing my Ph.D., I reached my final semester of school, and I was enthusiastic. In addition to being happy, I also felt a slight sense of insecurity. I had been in school for five years, had not worked full-time, and was approaching what I knew to be a normal life. I was unsure how I would feel as I had gotten so used to taking courses, spending at least six hours daily at the library reading research articles, editing drafts of my dissertation chapters, and meeting with Dr. Liz. Yet, it was time to prepare for my dissertation defense and graduation.

The dissertation defense is the last step in the Ph.D. process and consists of defending all five chapters. I like to think of the dissertation as a mini book. Chapter four is the analysis of data collection. Chapter five is the conclusion; it presents the author's thoughts about the results and future research that could be conducted. All chapters must be briefly presented to the committee, followed by questions from them to ensure the doctoral candidate can articulate their research well and think about additional information related to the topic. In addition to the committee, family and friends are welcome to attend. Having family and friends present was beneficial as I could showcase all the hard work I had been completing, and they could also ask questions to understand the research topic better. Furthermore, having their love and support was amazing.

April 12, 2021, arrived, and it was time to present my dissertation. I could hardly sleep the night before as I anticipated the experience and outcome of my dissertation defense. Although I attended three defenses—one in person and two virtually, every committee chair conducts their advisee's dissertation defense slightly differently.

I wanted to keep my nerves regulated when I woke up, so I prayed and worshiped God through song. Travis Greene "Made a Way," Smokie Norful's "Still Say Thank You," Todd Galberth's "Lord You are Good," and Marvin Sapp's "My Testimony" were my inspirations. Listening to and singing those songs helped calm me and keep me focused. I reflected on all my challenges and disappointments and how God brought me through. I definitely had a testimony and much to be thankful for. Many days, I thought I would not finish my degree; I wanted to give up. Despite it all, God allowed me to reach my dissertation defense day, and I was grateful.

My dissertation defense began virtually at 10 a.m., with Dr. Liz greeting me and welcoming my committee. She ensured we were all settled and ready before admitting my family and friends into the zoom meeting. My committee and I were ready, and the next thing I saw was smiling faces popping onto the screen. I was filled with mixed emotions—happiness, excitement, and nervousness because it was finally time to prove why I should earn the title Dr. Swope-Farr.

Dr. Liz greeted everyone and explained that I would begin by presenting my research topic, followed by questions from family, friends, and committee members. Then the committee would be placed in a breakout room so the committee could deliberate. I would be brought into the room with the committee to announce my fate—if I had passed or failed. Lastly, everyone would be brought back into the meeting to inform them of the outcome. Dr. Liz turned the meeting over to me, and the show began.

"Hello, everyone, and thanks for participating in my dissertation defense. The title of my research topic is, Examining Virtual Mathematics Instruction: A Comparative Case Study of In-service Elementary Teachers with Mathematics Anxiety and Math Teaching Self-Efficacy." Once I began introducing my research, the nervousness sailed away. I was in a zone and did very well articulating my information. When I finished, I solicited questions; most came from my committee members. Although I thought I would struggle to answer their questions, I responded proficiently and could tell based on their smiles and head nods.

As we sat in the waiting room for my committee to deliberate, many of my family and friends expressed how proud they were of me and gave congratulatory statements. I was so happy and filled with tears of joy from the love shown. I had no clue that so many people would make time to support me.

Although Dr. Liz did an excellent job prepping me for this day and told me that a committee should not allow a Ph.D. candidate to schedule a dissertation defense if they were not ready, I was still nervous about the outcome. The time had come for Dr. Liz to deliver the verdict; she brought me back into the meeting first and then announced the committee's decision. "You are officially Dr. Swope-Farr, so we want to bring everyone into the meeting." I was ecstatic that I was finally Dr. Swope-Farr. I expressed my deepest sentiments to my committee for their consistent love and support through the Ph.D. process.

To have a cohesive committee that supported me individually and collectively in their unique ways was a tremendous blessing. This cohesion was significant because I had heard several horror stories where committee members did not work well together, making it more challenging for the student. There were also students whose advisors left the university, leaving them to search for a replacement.

Even though I had an unpleasant experience with my old advisor, God blessed me with Dr. Liz and my outstanding committee members. I am ever grateful for their expertise, guidance, and assistance because obtaining a Ph.D. requires intense dedication, determination, time, courage, and confidence. I exemplified these virtues and more while earning my Ph.D.; they helped me realize that. I am incredibly proud of myself for persevering through all the circumstances, academically and personally. I give all praises and honor to God for carrying me through. I am a living witness of John 15:5 "I am the vine, you are the branches; the one who remains in Me, and I in him bears much fruit, for apart from Me you can do nothing" (NASB). I would have never made it had it not been for God giving me the courage and strength to get through each course, homework assignment, exam, and unpleasant occurrence.

Now that I am Dr. Swope-Farr, it took time for that title to sink in. When I heard someone address me as a doctor, it was at that moment I recalled that I was. Even a year later, it felt strange when I heard someone say Dr. Swope-Farr or introduce myself as such.

Chapter 6: Life After Ph.D.

"But if we hope for what we do not see, through perseverance we wait eagerly for it."
Romans 8:25(NASB)

Hope is anticipating something even when it appears that it may not happen. The blessing of having hope is that if one genuinely desires something, one will exhibit perseverance until one achieves what was hoped for. Oddly enough, sometimes you can wait for something so long that when it finally arrives, all the excitement you thought you would have and ideas about what you might do are different than what you anticipated.

After earning my Ph.D., I felt accomplished but felt a sense of skepticism about my career. While in school, I thought of becoming a consultant to assist high school students and families in preparing for post-secondary education, but I was not entirely sure what that big picture looked like. I even wondered if I could earn a reasonable living doing this and how I would apply what I learned while obtaining a doctorate. Further, when one achieves such a degree, many view them as esteemed experts in various concepts and having the ability to secure prestigious employment opportunities.

I desired to work full-time but also wanted time to rest my mind from pursuing my doctorate. Feeling a sense of urgency, I began applying for various leadership positions in MPS that would allow for work with coaching teachers and supporting or designing mathematics curricula. Engaging in work connected to these two areas could expand my existing knowledge to serve high school students' post-secondary needs and position me to gain access to high school families again. To my surprise, MPS did not invite me to any interviews. Other than a leadership position, the only option I was aware of was going back into the high school classroom to teach since math teachers were in great demand. But I knew I did not want to entertain that option; I sought a higher degree to access other options. As the summer concluded, I had no employment opportunities; thus, I was unsure if I would have a job at the start of the fall semester.

While searching an online recruitment site, I found two positions: a curriculum specialist in the Oconomowoc School District and a math interventionist at HSD. I applied for both, and HSD offered the position. Momentarily I felt I was settling for a position with pay well below what I could earn with my experience and education. However, I realized three things: a) I would be able to gain knowledge in an area I had not performed previously; b) I would be allowed to design and implement a program that broadens my expertise; c) the importance of being content and trusting God for my needs instead of focusing on income.

During my first year at HSD, I was needed to teach two freshmen-level courses. Initially, I was reluctant to teach, but students' needs always seemed to precede my desires. A few months into teaching, I was reminded why I left high school to pursue a doctorate. Having to spend more time managing behaviors than teaching math was stressful. Although teaching is my God-given gift, my passion for teaching began to diminish, and I felt a shift in my career aspirations. I could not verbalize those feelings, yet I knew it was time to change my line of work.

While conducting mock interviews with juniors, we began discussing their post-secondary plans. Some students expressed a desire to attend college but not necessarily go to the college of their dreams. Some mentioned they considered attending college but were unsure if they would pursue it. As the discussions unfolded, I was overwhelmed with excitement. I began to share some of my experiences choosing a school, attending college, and earning scholarships and fellowships to pay for college. These conversations confirmed my new calling—educating high school students and families about post-secondary education. This calling was not new per-say, but it became more evident while engaging with those students. I understood that motivating students to attend college, find a trade, or pursue a positive path that would make them successful adults was a natural part of my life.

"Motivationalist"

Years ago, I came across a poem by Marianne Williamson entitled "Our Deepest Fear," which positively impacted me. It motivated me to give my best to help anyone who desired to attend college. I often engage with individuals who desire to go to college but lack self-motivation and are fearful. The portion of her poem that stood out the most was:

> "We ask ourselves, who am I to be brilliant, gorgeous, talented, fabulous? Actually, who are you not to be? You are a child of God… As we let our own Light shine, we consciously give other people permission to do the same. As we are liberated from our own fear, our presence automatically liberates others."

Often as individuals, we do not live to our fullest potential. We second guess our abilities, knowledge, worth, and skills, not realizing how important those attributes are for inspiring and uplifting others. With that, I had not grasped how I had inspired others and how significant my experiences were to my family, friends, students, and church family. Earning a Ph.D. influenced me and many people I had relationships with.

During my graduation dinner, I was stunned by the number of people who shared stories of how I inspired them through my educational journey. I learned that the life I had been living had meaning, and I must continue to allow God to use me to motivate and encourage whoever crossed my path. I can confidently say I am an excellent example of a Black woman for young black girls who desire to set goals, achieve them, and live a magnificent life. More importantly, being such an example is showcased through my actions, not just my speech, for through the life I live, I excite others. We certainly need role models for our youth. Youth need to see individuals who look like them succeeding, achieving the unachievable, and transforming society.

Conclusion

Dream big little one; dream many dreams. Develop a plan and set goals, for you'll never know where you might land. Life brings many obstacles; look for the lessons they leave. Utilize all opportunities set before you; each moves you closer to your dreams. There will be days when you're running, days when you're crawling, and days when you're walking, but let nothing hinder your stride. Know that your dreams are waiting patiently; your journey is designing the blueprint for them. No matter when you achieve your dreams, know that God is transporting you.

My dream was fulfilled, yet not precisely how and when I planned it. Through various trials, I never gave up or lost sight of it because God was molding, strengthening, and preparing me every step of the way. He said, "I know the plans I have for you, plans to prosper you and not harm you, plans to give you hope and a future" Jeremiah 29:11 (NASB). Little did I know all the challenges and difficulties produced a testimony to be a blessing and comfort to others.

My mathematical journey has been one I would not change. The roller coaster rides, disappointments, and excitement all worked out for my good. This expedition was designed and assigned to me to encourage and motivate others. A trailblazer is what I became by setting the bar and paving the way for those who'll come after me. Becoming the first black individual to earn a Ph.D. in urban education- mathematics education at a research one university was a blessing. I aim to make myself available for young boys and girls to accomplish great things. I am an innovator, so others will not struggle, be uninformed, or lack a role model who looks like them. I develop math aces and will continue until I die.

You can see dreams from a little girl paid off. Although I did not know what it took to become Dr. Swope, I figured it out personally and academically through various trials. Hence, dream big and prevent difficulties from hindering your heart's desires. Sometimes, a door is closed, yet see what can be learned from that experience. "Rejection comes from people who don't think you belong; rejection is not failure, it's a calibrator, it can help you learn who you are and what you want" Colin Kaepernick. I can't be sure if some professors believed I did not belong; their actions gave that impression. On the contrary, I realized my terrible experiences revealed God's strength in me and showed me that I am needed in the education field to support others.

I hope this book was informative for all readers and a tool to admonish individuals to follow their aspirations. There are occasions when we face stumbling blocks that make us lose hope, but during those times, we must reflect on our purpose, reassure ourselves, and seek guidance to regain that hope. When flying high and life is at ease, we must remember to share the wealth, reach back to help someone, and be grateful because God is our guide, strength, peace, comfort, and provider.

About the Author

Telashay Swope-Farr is an ambitious educator passionate about developing an understanding of mathematics and preparing students for post-secondary education and careers. She serves various populations of students from secondary to post-secondary education at public and private institutions. Swope-Farr is an innovative leader, a passionate educator, and a woman of influence.

She received awards for Mathematics Teacher of the year, Metropolitan Milwaukee Alliance of Black School Educators, Emerging Leader, Innovator Teacher, Most Valuable Teacher, and the Women's Achievement Award. She was a featured graduate student at the University of Wisconsin-Milwaukee for the Advance Opportunity Fellowship program.

Dr. Swope-Farr is an assistant professor and educational consultant. When she is not cultivating others' mathematical abilities, she spends quality time with her family, serves her church in various capacities, and reads her Bible.

This book is Dr. Swope-Farr's first solo book debut, and she anticipates writing more books that will be informative for younger generations and individuals in the education community.

Acknowledgments

First, thank God for predestining me with the gift of teaching and understanding mathematics. Without Him, I am nothing and can do nothing. I want to thank the math teachers that helped develop my mathematical abilities: Mrs. Karim-Tipton, Mr. Giles, Mrs. Kubinski, Mr. McCoy, and Dr. Willenbring. I am incredibly grateful to Mr. McCoy for all his continued love and support after graduating from Rust College. I appreciate Dr. Liz Drame; she is one of my guardian angels, and her wisdom is unmatchable. I appreciate the time she put into writing the foreword for this book.

I want to thank my husband, Apelles, and daughter, Assyria, for their patience and love for me while pursuing my doctorate. Thanks to my cousin Brandon (Scooter) for recognizing my math skills in high school; I did not know I was talented in math then. I am grateful to my sister, Carlaseea Shannon, for designing my book cover. Last, I am indebted to my amazing mother, Lisa Marks, for my upbringing and for giving up her future for me; I will always love her for that.

Made in the USA
Coppell, TX
26 November 2023